PENGUIN BOOKS — GREAT IDEAS
Silly Novels by Lady Novelists

D0531093

George Eliot

(1819–1880)

George Eliot

Silly Novels by Lady Novelists

PENGUIN BOOKS — GREAT IDEAS

PENGUIN BOOKS

Published by the Penguin Group
Penguin Books Ltd, 80 Strand, London WC2R ORL, England
Penguin Group (USA) Inc., 375 Hudson Street, New York, New York 10014, USA
Penguin Group (Canada), 90 Eglinton Avenue East, Suite 700, Toronto, Ontario, Canada M4P 2Y3
(a division of Pearson Penguin Canada Inc.)
Penguin Ireland, 25 St Stephen's Green, Dublin 2, Ireland (a division of Penguin Books Ltd)
Penguin Group (Australia), 250 Camberwell Road, Camberwell, Victoria 3124, Australia
(a division of Pearson Australia Group Pty Ltd)
Penguin Books India Pvt Ltd, 11 Community Centre, Panchsheel Park,
New Delhi – 110 017, India
Penguin Group (NZ), 67 Apollo Drive, Rosedale, North Shore 0632, New Zealand
(a division of Pearson New Zealand Ltd)
Penguin Books (South Africa) (Pty) Ltd, 24 Sturdee Avenue, Rosebank, Johannesburg 2196,
South Africa

Penguin Books Ltd, Registered Offices: 80 Strand, London WC2R ORL, England

www.penguin.com

This selection published in Penguin Books 2010

1

All rights reserved

Set in 11/13 Dante MT Std
Typeset by TexTech International
Printed in England by Clays Ltd, St Ives plc

ISBN: 978-0-141-19275-8

www.greenpenguin.co.uk

Contents

Silly Novels by Lady Novelists

Silly novels by Lady Novelists are a genus with many species, determined by the particular quality of silliness that
predominates in them – the frothy, the prosy, the pious,
or the pedantic. But it is a mixture of all these – a com-
posite order of feminine fatuity, that produces the largest
class of such novels, which we shall distinguish as the
mind-and-millinery species. The heroine is usually an heiress, probably a peeress in her own right, with perhaps
a vicious baronet, an amiable duke, and an irresistible
younger son of a marquis as lovers in the foreground, a
clergyman and a poet sighing for her in the middle distance, and a crowd of undefined adorers dimly indicated
beyond. Her eyes and her wit are both dazzling; her nose
and her morals are alike free from any tendency to irregu-
larity; she has a superb *contralto* and a superb intellect;
she is perfectly well-dressed and perfectly religious; she
dances like a sylph, and reads the Bible in the original
tongues. Or it may be that the heroine is not an heiress –
that rank and wealth are the only things in which she is
deficient; but she infallibly gets into high society, she has
the triumph of refusing many matches and securing the
best, and she wears some family jewels or other as a sort
of crown of righteousness at the end. Rakish men either
bite their lips in impotent confusion at her repartees,
or are touched to penitence by her reproofs, which, on

appropriate occasions, rise to a lofty strain of rhetoric; indeed, there is a general propensity in her to make speeches, and to rhapsodize at some length when she retires to her bedroom. In her recorded conversations she is amazingly eloquent, and in her unrecorded conversations, amazingly witty. She is understood to have a depth of insight that looks through and through the shallow theories of philosophers, and her superior instincts are a sort of dial by which men have only to set their clocks and watches, and all will go well. The men play a very subordinate part by her side. You are consoled now and then by a hint that they have affairs, which keeps you in mind that the working-day business of the world is some-how being carried on, but ostensibly the final cause of their existence is that they may accompany the heroine on her 'starring' expedition through life. They see her at a ball, and are dazzled; at a flower-show, and they are fas-cinated; on a riding excursion, and they are witched by her noble horsemanship; at church, and they are awed by the sweet solemnity of her demeanour. She is the ideal woman in feelings, faculties, and flounces. For all this, she as often as not marries the wrong person to begin with, and she suffers terribly from the plots and intrigues of the vicious baronet; but even death has a soft place in his heart for such a paragon, and remedies all mistakes for her just at the right moment. The vicious baronet is sure to be killed in a duel, and the tedious husband dies in his bed, requesting his wife, as a particular favour to him, to marry the man she loves best, and having already dispatched a note to the lover informing him of the comfortable arrangement. Before matters arrive at this desirable issue our feelings are tried by seeing the noble, lovely, and gifted heroine pass through many *mauvais moments*, but we have the satisfaction of knowing that her sorrows are wept into embroidered pocket-handkerchiefs, that her fainting form reclines on the very best upholstery, and that whatever vicissitudes she may undergo, from being dashed out of her carriage to having her head shaved in a fever, she comes out of them all with a complexion more blooming and locks more redundant than ever.

We may remark, by the way, that we have been relieved from a serious scruple by discovering that silly novels by lady novelists rarely introduce us into any other than very lofty and fashionable society. We had imagined that destitute women turned novelists, as they turned governesses, because they had no other 'lady-like' means of getting their bread. On this supposition, vacillating syntax and improbable incident had a certain pathos for us, like the extremely supererogatory pincushions and ill-devised nightcaps that are offered for sale by a blind man. We felt the commodity to be a nuisance, but we were glad to think that the money went to relieve the necessitous, and we pictured to ourselves lonely women struggling for a maintenance, or wives and daughters devoting themselves to the production of 'copy' out of pure heroism, – perhaps to pay their husband's debts, or to purchase luxuries for a sick father. Under these impressions we shrank from criticizing a lady's novel: her English might be faulty, but, we said to ourselves, her motives are irreproachable; her imagination may be uninventive, but her patience is untiring. Empty writing was excused by an empty stomach, and twaddle was consecrated by tears. But no! This theory of ours, like many other pretty theories, has had to give way before observation. Women's silly novels, we are now convinced, are written under totally different circumstances. The fair writers have evidently never talked to a tradesman except from a carriage window; they have no notion of the working classes except as 'dependants'; they think £500 a year a miserable pittance; Belgravia and 'baronial halls' are their primary truths; and they have no idea of feeling interest in any man who is not at least a great landed proprietor, if not a prime minister. It is clear that they write in elegant boudoirs, with violet-coloured ink and a ruby pen; that they must be entirely indifferent to publishers' accounts, and inexperienced in every form of poverty except poverty of brains. It is true that we are constantly struck with the want of verisimilitude in their representations of the high society in which they seem to live; but then they betray no closer acquaintance with any other form of life. If their peers and peeresses are improbable, their literary men, tradespeople, and cottagers are impossible; and their intellect seems to have the peculiar impartiality of reproducing both what they *have* seen and heard, and what they have *not* seen and heard, with equal unfaithfulness.

There are few women, we suppose, who have not seen something of children under five years of age, yet in *Compensation*, a recent novel of the mind-and-millinery species, which calls itself a 'story of real life', we have a child of four and a half years old talking in this Ossianic fashion: –

'Oh, I am so happy, dear gran'mamma; – I have seen, – I have seen such a delightful person: he is like everything beautiful, – like the smell of sweet flowers, and the view from Ben Lomond; – or no, *better than that* – he is like what I think of and see when I am very, very happy; and he is really like mamma, too, when she sings; and his forehead is like *that distant sea*,' she continued, pointing to the blue Mediterranean; 'there seems no end – no end; or like the clusters of stars I like best to look at on a warm fine night . . . Don't look so . . . your forehead is like Loch Lomond, when the wind is blowing and the sun is gone in; I like the sunshine best when the lake is smooth . . . So now – I like it better than ever . . . it is more beautiful still from the dark cloud that has gone over it, *when the sun suddenly lights up all the colours of the forests and shining purple rocks, and it is all reflected in the waters below.*'

We are not surprised to learn that the mother of this infant phenomenon, who exhibits symptoms so alarmingly like those of adolescence repressed by gin, is herself a phœnix. We are assured, again and again, that she had a remarkably original mind, that she was a genius, and 'conscious of her originality', and she was fortunate enough to have a lover who was also a genius, and a man of 'most original mind'.

This lover, we read, though 'wonderfully similar' to her 'in powers and capacity', was 'infinitely superior to her in faith and development', and she saw in him the '"Agape" – so rare to find – of which she had read and admired the meaning in her Greek Testament; having, *from her great facility in learning languages*, read the Scriptures in their original *tongues*.' Of course! Greek and Hebrew are mere play to a heroine; Sanscrit is no more than *a b c* to her; and she can talk with perfect correctness in any language except English. She is a polking polyglot, a Creuzer in crinoline. Poor men! There are so few of you who know even Hebrew; you think it something to boast of if, like Bolingbroke, you only 'understand that sort of learning, and what is writ about it'; and you are perhaps adoring women who can think slightingly of you in all the Semitic languages successively. But, then, as we are almost invariably told, that a heroine has a 'beautifully small head', and as her intellect has probably been early invigorated by an attention to costume and deportment, we may conclude that she can pick up the Oriental tongues, to say nothing of their dialects, with the same aërial facility that the butterfly sips nectar. Besides, there can be no difficulty in conceiving the depth of the heroine's erudition, when that of the authoress is so evident.

In *Laura Gay*, another novel of the same school, the heroine seems less at home in Greek and Hebrew, but she makes up for the deficiency by a quite playful familiarity with the Latin classics – with the 'dear old Virgil', 'the graceful Horace, the humane Cicero, and the pleasant Livy'; indeed, it is such a matter of course with her to quote Latin, that she does it at a picnic in a very mixed company of ladies and gentlemen, having, we are told, 'no conception that the nobler sex were capable of jealousy on this subject. And if, indeed,' continues the biographer of Laura Gay, 'the wisest and noblest portion of that sex were in the majority, no such sentiment would exist; but while Miss Wyndhams and Mr Redfords abound, great sacrifices must be made to their existence.' Such sacrifices, we presume, as abstaining from Latin quotations, of extremely moderate interest and applicability, which the wise and noble minority of the other sex would be quite as willing to dispense with as the foolish and ignoble majority. It is as little the custom of well-bred men as of well-bred women to quote Latin in mixed parties; they can contain their familiarity with 'the humane Cicero' without allowing it to boil over in ordinary conversation, and even references to 'the pleasant Livy' are not absolutely irrepressible. But Ciceronian Latin is the mildest form of Miss Gay's conversational power. Being on the Palatine with a party of sightseers, she falls into the following vein of well-rounded remark: –

> Truth can only be pure objectively, for even in the creeds where it predominates, being subjective, and parcelled out into portions, each of these necessarily receives a hue of idiosyncrasy, that is, a taint of superstition more or less strong; while in such creeds as the Roman Catholic, ignorance, interest, the bias of ancient idolatries, and the force of authority, have gradually accumulated on the pure truth, and transformed it, at last, into a mass of superstition for the majority of its votaries; and how few are there, alas! whose zeal, courage, and intellectual energy are equal to the analysis of this accumulation, and to the discovery of the pearl of great price which lies hidden beneath this heap of rubbish.

We have often met with women much more novel and profound in their observations than Laura Gay, but rarely with any so inopportunely long-winded. A clerical lord, who is half in love with her, is alarmed by the daring remarks just quoted, and begins to suspect that she is inclined to free-thinking. But he is mistaken; when in a moment of sorrow he delicately begs leave to 'recall to her memory, a *dépôt* of strength and consolation under affliction, which, until we are hard pressed by the trials of life, we are too apt to forget', we learn that she really has 'recurrence to that sacred *dépôt*', together with the tea-pot. There is a certain flavour of orthodoxy mixed with the parade of fortunes and fine carriages in *Laura Gay*, but it is an orthodoxy mitigated by study of 'the humane Cicero', and by an 'intellectual disposition to analyse'.

Compensation is much more heavily dosed with doctrine, but then it has a treble amount of snobbish worldliness and absurd incident to tickle the palate of pious frivolity. Linda, the heroine, is still more speculative and spiritual than Laura Gay, but she has been 'presented', and has more, and far grander, lovers; very wicked and fascinating women are introduced – even a French *lionne*; and no expense is spared to get up as exciting a story as you will find in the most immoral novels. In fact, it is a wonderful *pot pourri* of Almack's, Scotch second-sight, Mr Rogers's breakfasts, Italian brigands, death-bed conversions, superior authoresses, Italian mistresses, and attempts at poisoning old ladies, the whole served up with a garnish of talk about 'faith and development', and 'most original minds'. Even Miss Susan Barton, the superior authoress, whose pen moves in a 'quick decided manner when she is composing', declines the finest opportunities of marriage; and though old enough to be Linda's mother (since we are told that she refused Linda's father), has her hand sought by a young earl, the heroine's rejected lover.

Of course, genius and morality must be backed by eligible offers, or they would seem rather a dull affair; and piety, like other things, in order to be *comme il faut*, must be in 'society', and have admittance to the best circles.

Rank and Beauty is a more frothy and less religious variety of the mind-and-millinery species. The heroine, we are told, 'if she inherited her father's pride of birth and her mother's beauty of person, had in herself a tone of enthusiastic feeling that perhaps belongs to her age even in the lowly born, but which is refined into the high spirit of wild romance only in the far descended, who feel that it is their best inheritance'. This enthusiastic young lady, by dint of reading the newspaper to her father, falls in love with the *prime minister*, who, through the medium of leading articles and 'the *résumé* of the debates', shines upon her imagination as a bright particular star, which has no parallax for her, living in the country as simple Miss Wyndham. But she forthwith becomes Baroness Umfraville in her own right, astonishes the world with her beauty and accomplishments when she bursts upon it from her mansion in Spring Gardens, and, as you foresee, will presently come into contact with the unseen *objet aimé*. Perhaps the words 'prime minister' suggest to you a wrinkled or obese sexagenarian; but pray dismiss the image. Lord Rupert Conway has been 'called while still almost a youth to the first situation which a subject can hold in the *universe*', and even leading articles and a *résumé* of the debates have not conjured up a dream that surpasses the fact.

The door opened again, and Lord Rupert Conway entered. Evelyn gave one glance. It was enough; she was not disappointed. It seemed as if a picture on which she had long gazed was suddenly instinct with life, and had stepped from its frame before her. His tall figure, the distinguished simplicity of his air – it was a living Vandyke, a cavalier, one of his noble cavalier ancestors, or one to whom her fancy had always likened him, who long of yore had, with an Umfraville, fought the Paynim far beyond sea. Was this reality?

Very little like it, certainly.

By and by, it becomes evident that the ministerial heart is touched. Lady Umfraville is on a visit to the Queen at Windsor, and, –

The last evening of her stay, when they returned from riding, Mr Wyndham took her and a large party to the top of the Keep, to see the view. She was leaning on the battlements, gazing from that 'stately height' at the prospect beneath her, when Lord Rupert was by her side. 'What an unrivalled view!' exclaimed she.

'Yes, it would have been wrong to go without having been up here. You are pleased with your visit?'

'Enchanted! "A Queen to live and die under", to live and die for!'

'Ha!' cried he, with sudden emotion, and with a *eureka* expression of countenance, as if he had *indeed found a heart in unison with his own*.

The '*eureka* expression of countenance', you see at once to be prophetic of marriage at the end of the third volume; but before that desirable consummation, there are very complicated misunderstandings, arising chiefly from the vindictive plotting of Sir Luttrell Wycherley, who is a genius, a poet, and in every way a most remarkable character indeed. He is not only a romantic poet, but a hardened rake and a cynical wit; yet his deep passion for Lady Umfraville has so impoverished his epigrammatic talent, that he cuts an extremely poor figure in conversation. When she rejects him, he rushes into the shrubbery, and rolls himself in the dirt; and on recovering, devotes himself to the most diabolical and laborious schemes of vengeance, in the course of which he disguises himself as a quack physician, and enters into general practice, foreseeing that Evelyn will fall ill, and that he shall be called in to attend her. At last, when all his schemes are frustrated, he takes leave of her in a long letter, written, as you will perceive from the following passage, entirely in the style of an eminent literary man: –

Oh, lady, nursed in pomp and pleasure, will you ever cast one thought upon the miserable being who addresses you? Will you ever, as your gilded galley is floating down the unruffled stream of prosperity, will you ever, while lulled by the sweetest music – thine own praises, – hear the far-off sigh from that world to which I am going?

On the whole, however, frothy as it is, we rather prefer *Rank and Beauty* to the two other novels we have mentioned. The dialogue is more natural and spirited; there is some frank ignorance, and no pedantry; and you are allowed to take the heroine's astounding intellect upon trust, without being called on to read her conversational refutations of sceptics and philosophers, or her rhetorical solutions of the mysteries of the universe.

Writers of the mind-and-millinery school are remarkably unanimous in their choice of diction. In their novels, there is usually a lady or gentleman who is more or less of a upas tree: the lover has a manly breast; minds are redolent of various things; hearts are hollow; events are utilized; friends are consigned to the tomb; infancy is an engaging period; the sun is a luminary that goes to his western couch, or gathers the rain-drops into his refulgent bosom; life is a melancholy boon; Albion and Scotia are conversational epithets. There is a striking resemblance, too, in the character of their moral comments, such, for instance, as that 'It is a fact, no less true than melancholy, that all people, more or less, richer or poorer, are swayed by bad example'; that 'Books, however trivial, contain some subjects from which useful information may be drawn'; that 'Vice can too often borrow the language of virtue'; that 'Merit and nobility of nature must exist, to be accepted, for clamour and pretension cannot impose upon those too well read in human nature to be easily deceived'; and that, 'In order to forgive, we must have been injured'. There is, doubtless, a class of readers to whom these remarks appear peculiarly pointed and pungent; for we often find them doubly and trebly scored with the pencil, and delicate hands giving in their determined adhesion to these hardy novelties by a distinct *très vrai*, emphasized by many notes of exclamation. The colloquial style of these novels is often marked by much ingenious inversion, and a careful avoidance of such cheap phraseology as can be heard every day. Angry young gentlemen exclaim – "'Tis ever thus, methinks'; and in the half hour before dinner a young lady informs her next neighbour that the first day she read Shakspeare she 'stole away into the park, and beneath the shadow of the greenwood tree, devoured with rapture the inspired page of the great magician'. But the most remarkable efforts of the mind-and-millinery writers lie in their philosophic reflections. The authoress of *Laura Gay*, for example, having married her hero and heroine, improves the event by observing that 'if those sceptics, whose eyes have so long gazed on matter that they can no longer see aught else in man, could once enter with heart and soul into such bliss as this, they would come to say that the soul of man and the polypus are not of common origin, or of the same texture'. Lady novelists, it appears, can see something else besides matter; they are not limited to phenomena, but can relieve their eyesight by occasional glimpses of the *noumenon*, and are, therefore, naturally better able than any one else to confound sceptics, even of that remarkable, but to us unknown school, which maintains that the soul of man is of the same texture as the polypus.

The most pitiable of all silly novels by lady novelists are what we may call the *oracular* species – novels intended to expound the writer's religious, philosophical, or moral theories. There seems to be a notion abroad among women, rather akin to the superstition that the speech and actions of idiots are inspired, and that the human being most entirely exhausted of common sense is the fittest vehicle of revelation. To judge from their writings, there are certain ladies who think that an amazing ignorance, both of science and of life, is the best possible qualification for

forming an opinion on the knottiest moral and speculative questions. Apparently, their recipe for solving all such
difficulties is something like this: – Take a woman's head,
stuff it with a smattering of philosophy and literature
chopped small, and with false notions of society baked
hard, let it hang over a desk a few hours every day, and
serve up hot in feeble English, when not required. You
will rarely meet with a lady novelist of the oracular class
who is diffident of her ability to decide on theological
questions, – who has any suspicion that she is not capable
of discriminating with the nicest accuracy between the
good and evil in all church parties, – who does not see
precisely how it is that men have gone wrong hitherto, –
and pity philosophers in general that they have not had
the opportunity of consulting her. Great writers, who
have modestly contented themselves with putting their
experience into fiction, and have thought it quite a sufficient task to exhibit men and things as they are, she sighs
over as deplorably deficient in the application of their
powers. 'They have solved no great questions' – and she
is ready to remedy their omission by setting before you a
complete theory of life and manual of divinity, in a love
story, where ladies and gentlemen of good family go
through genteel vicissitudes, to the utter confusion of
Deists, Puseyites, and ultra-Protestants, and to the perfect establishment of that particular view of Christianity
which either condenses itself into a sentence of small
caps, or explodes into a cluster of stars on the three hundred and thirtieth page. It is true, the ladies and gentlemen will probably seem to you remarkably little like any
you have had the fortune or misfortune to meet with, for,

as a general rule, the ability of a lady novelist to describe actual life and her fellow-men, is in inverse proportion to her confident eloquence about God and the other world, and the means by which she usually chooses to conduct you to true ideas of the invisible is a totally false picture of the visible.

As typical a novel of the oracular kind as we can hope to meet with, is *The Enigma: A Leaf from the Chronicles of Wolchorley House*. The 'enigma' which this novel is to solve, is certainly one that demands powers no less gigantic than those of a lady novelist, being neither more nor less than the existence of evil. The problem is stated, and the answer dimly foreshadowed on the very first page. The spirited young lady, with raven hair, says, 'All life is an inextricable confusion'; and the meek young lady, with auburn hair, looks at the picture of the Madonna which she is copying, and – '*There* seemed the solution of that mighty enigma.' The style of this novel is quite as lofty as its purpose; indeed, some passages on which we have spent much patient study are quite beyond our reach, in spite of the illustrative aid of italics and small caps; and we must await further 'development' in order to understand them. Of Ernest, the model young clergyman, who sets every one right on all occasions, we read, that 'he held not of marriage in the marketable kind, after a social desecration'; that, on one eventful night, 'sleep had not visited his divided heart, where tumultuated, in varied type and combination, the aggregate feelings of grief and joy'; and that, 'for the *marketable* human article he had no toleration, be it of what sort, or set for what value it might, whether for worship or class, his upright soul abhorred it, whose ultimatum, the self-deceiver, was to him THE *great spiritual lie*, "living in a vain show, deceiving and being deceived"; since he did not suppose the phylactery and enlarged border on the garment to be *merely* a social trick.' (The italics and small caps are the author's, and we hope they assist the reader's comprehension.) Of Sir Lionel, the model old gentleman, we are told that 'the simple ideal of the middle age, apart from its anarchy and decadence, in him most truly seemed to live again, when the ties which knit men together were of heroic cast. The first-born colours of pristine faith and truth engraven on the common soul of man, and blent into the wide arch of brotherhood, where the primæval law of *order* grew and multiplied, each perfect after his kind, and mutually interdependent.' You see clearly, of course, how colours are first engraven on a soul, and then blent into a wide arch, on which arch of colours – apparently a rainbow – the law of order grew and multiplied, each – apparently the arch and the law – perfect after his kind? If, after this, you can possibly want any further aid towards knowing what Sir Lionel was, we can tell you, that in his soul 'the scientific combinations of thought could educe no fuller harmonies of the good and the true, than lay in the primæval pulses which floated as an atmosphere around it!' and that, when he was sealing a letter, 'Lo! the responsive throb in that good man's bosom echoed back in simple truth the honest witness of a heart that condemned him not, as his eye, bedewed with love, rested, too, with something of ancestral pride, on the undimmed motto of the family – LOIAUTÉ.'

The slightest matters have their vulgarity fumigated out

of them by the same elevated style. Commonplace people would say that a copy of Shakspeare lay on a drawing-room table; but the authoress of *The Enigma*, bent on edifying periphrasis, tells you that there lay on the table, 'that fund of human thought and feeling, which teaches the heart through the little name, "Shakspeare"'. A watchman sees a light burning in an upper window rather longer than usual, and thinks that people are foolish to sit up late when they have an opportunity of going to bed; but, lest this fact should seem too low and common, it is presented to us in the following striking and metaphysical manner: 'He marvelled – as man *will* think for others in a necessarily separate personality, consequently (though disallowing it) in false mental premise, – how differently *he* should act, how gladly *he* should prize the rest so lightly held of within.' A footman – an ordinary Jeames, with large calves and aspirated vowels – answers the door-bell, and the opportunity is seized to tell you that he was a 'type of the large class of pampered menials, who follow the curse of Cain – "vagabonds" on the face of the earth, and whose estimate of the human class varies in the graduated scale of money and expenditure . . . These, and such as these, O England, be the false lights of thy morbid civilization!' We have heard of various 'false lights', from Dr Cumming to Robert Owen, from Dr Pusey to the Spirit-rappers, but we never before heard of the false light that emanates from plush and powder.

In the same way very ordinary events of civilized life are exalted into the most awful crises, and ladies in full skirts and *manches à la chinoise*, conduct themselves not unlike the heroines of sanguinary melodramas. Mrs Percy, a shallow woman of the world, wishes her son Horace to marry the auburn-haired Grace, she being an heiress; but he, after the manner of sons, falls in love with the raven-haired Kate, the heiress's portionless cousin; and, moreover, Grace herself shows every symptom of perfect indifference to Horace. In such cases, sons are often sulky or fiery, mothers are alternately manœuvring and waspish, and the portionless young lady often lies awake at night and cries a good deal. We are getting used to these things now, just as we are used to eclipses of the moon, which no longer set us howling and beating tin kettles. We never heard of a lady in a fashionable 'front' behaving like Mrs Percy under these circumstances. Happening one day to see Horace talking to Grace at a window, without in the least knowing what they are talking about, or having the least reason to believe that Grace, who is mistress of the house and a person of dignity, would accept her son if he were to offer himself, she suddenly rushes up to them and clasps them both, saying, 'with a flushed countenance and in an excited manner' – 'This is indeed happiness; for, may I not call you so, Grace? – my Grace – my Horace's Grace! – my dear children!' Her son tells her she is mistaken, and that he is engaged to Kate, whereupon we have the following scene and tableau: –

Gathering herself up to an unprecedented height, (!) her eyes lightning forth the fire of her anger: –

'Wretched boy!' she said, hoarsely and scornfully, and clenching her hand. 'Take then the doom of your own choice! Bow down your miserable head and let a mother's –'

'Curse not!' spake a deep low voice from behind, and Mrs Percy started, scared, as though she had seen a heavenly visitant appear, to break upon her in the midst of her sin.

Meantime, Horace had fallen on his knees at her feet, and hid his face in his hands.

Who, then, is she – who! Truly his 'guardian spirit' hath stepped between him and the fearful words, which, however unmerited, must have hung as a pall over his future existence; – a spell which could not be unbound – which could not be unsaid.

Of an earthly paleness, but calm with the still, iron-bound calmness of death – the only calm one there, – Katherine stood; and her words smote on the ear in tones whose appallingly slow and separate intonation rung on the heart like the chill, isolated tolling of some fatal knell.

'He would have plighted me his faith, but I did not accept it; you cannot, therefore – you *dare* not curse him. And here,' she continued, raising her hand to heaven, whither her large dark eyes also rose with a chastened glow, which, for the first time, *suffering* had lighted in those passionate orbs, – 'here I promise, come weal, come woe, that Horace Wolchorley and I do never interchange vows without his mother's sanction – without his mother's blessing!'

Here, and throughout the story, we see that confusion of purpose which is so characteristic of silly novels written by women. It is a story of quite modern drawing-room society – a society in which polkas are played and

Puseyism discussed; yet we have characters, and incidents, and traits of manner introduced, which are mere shreds from the most heterogeneous romances. We have a blind Irish harper, 'relic of the picturesque bards of yore', startling us at a Sunday-school festival of tea and cake in an English village; we have a crazy gypsy, in a scarlet cloak, singing snatches of romantic song, and revealing a secret on her death-bed which, with the testimony of a dwarfish miserly merchant, who salutes strangers with a curse and a devilish laugh, goes to prove that Ernest, the model young clergyman, is Kate's brother; and we have an ultra-virtuous Irish Barney, discovering that a document is forged, by comparing the date of the paper with the date of the alleged signature, although the same document has passed through a court of law, and occasioned a fatal decision. The 'Hall' in which Sir Lionel lives is the venerable country-seat of an old family, and this, we suppose, sets the imagination of the authoress flying to donjons and battlements, where 'lo! the warder blows his horn'; for, as the inhabitants are in their bedrooms on a night certainly within the recollection of Pleaceman X., and a breeze springs up, which we are at first told was faint, and then that it made the old cedars bow their branches to the greensward, she falls into this mediæval vein of description (the italics are ours): 'The banner *unfurled it* at the sound, and shook its guardian wing above, while the startled owl *flapped her* in the ivy; the firmament looking down through her "argus eyes" –

Ministers of heaven's mute melodies.

And lo! two strokes tolled from out the warder tower, and "Two o'clock" re-echoed its interpreter below.'

Such stories as this of *The Enigma* remind us of the pictures clever children sometimes draw 'out of their own head', where you will see a modern villa on the right, two knights in helmets fighting in the foreground, and a tiger grinning in a jungle on the left, the several objects being brought together because the artist thinks each pretty, and perhaps still more because he remembers seeing them in other pictures.

But we like the authoress much better on her mediæval stilts than on her oracular ones, – when she talks of the *Ich* and of 'subjective' and 'objective', and lays down the exact line of Christian verity, between 'right-hand excesses and left-hand declensions'. Persons who deviate from this line are introduced with a patronizing air of charity. Of a certain Miss Inshquine she informs us, with all the lucidity of italics and small caps, that '*function*, not *form*, AS THE INEVITABLE OUTER EXPRESSION OF THE SPIRIT IN THIS TABERNACLED AGE, weakly engrossed her'. And *à propos* of Miss Mayjar, an evangelical lady who is a little too apt to talk of her visits to sick women and the state of their souls, we are told that the model clergyman is 'not one to disallow, through the *super* crust, the undercurrent towards good in the *subject*, or the positive benefits, nevertheless, to the *object*'. We imagine the double-refined accent and protrusion of chin which are feebly represented by the italics in this lady's sentences. We abstain from quoting any of her oracular doctrinal passages, because they refer to matters too serious for our pages just now.

The epithet 'silly' may seem impertinent, applied to a novel which indicates so much reading and intellectual activity as *The Enigma*; but we use this epithet advisedly. If, as the world has long agreed, a very great amount of instruction will not make a wise man, still less will a very mediocre amount of instruction make a wise woman. And the most mischievous form of feminine silliness is the literary form, because it tends to confirm the popular prejudice against the more solid education of women. When men see girls wasting their time in consultations about bonnets and ball dresses, and in giggling or senti- mental love-confidences, or middle-aged women misman- aging their children, and solacing themselves with acrid gossip, they can hardly help saying, 'For Heaven's sake, let girls be better educated; let them have some better objects of thought – some more solid occupations.' But after a few hours' conversation with an oracular literary woman, or a few hours' reading of her books, they are likely enough to say, 'After all, when a woman gets some knowledge, see what use she makes of it! Her knowledge remains acquisition, instead of passing into culture; in- stead of being subdued into modesty and simplicity by a larger acquaintance with thought and fact, she has a feverish consciousness of her attainments; she keeps a sort of mental pocket-mirror, and is continually looking in it at her own 'intellectuality'; she spoils the taste of one's muffin by questions of metaphysics; 'puts down' men at a dinner-table with her superior information; and seizes the opportunity of a *soirée* to catechize us on the vital question of the relation between mind and matter. And then, look at her writings! She mistakes vagueness for depth, bombast for eloquence, and affectation for originality; she struts on one page, rolls her eyes on another, grimaces in a third, and is hysterical in a fourth. She may have read many writings of great men, and a few writings of great women; but she is as unable to discern the difference between her own style and theirs as a Yorkshireman is to discern the difference between his own English and a Londoner's: rhodomontade is the native accent of her intellect. No – the average nature of women is too shallow and feeble a soil to bear much tillage; it is only fit for the very lightest crops.'

It is true that the men who come to such a decision on such very superficial and imperfect observation may not be among the wisest in the world; but we have not now to contest their opinion – we are only pointing out how it is unconsciously encouraged by many women who have volunteered themselves as representatives of the feminine intellect. We do not believe that a man was ever strengthened in such an opinion by associating with a woman of true culture, whose mind had absorbed her knowledge instead of being absorbed by it. A really cultured woman, like a really cultured man, is all the simpler and the less obtrusive for her knowledge; it has made her see herself and her opinions in something like just proportions; she does not make it a pedestal from which she flatters herself that she commands a complete view of men and things, but makes it a point of observation from which to form a right estimate of herself. She neither spouts poetry nor quotes Cicero on slight provocation; not because she thinks that a sacrifice must be made to the prejudices of men, but because that mode of exhibiting her memory and Latinity does not present itself to her as edifying or graceful. She does not write books to confound philosophers, perhaps because she is able to write books that delight them. In conversation she is the least formidable of women, because she understands you, without wanting to make you aware that you *can't* understand her. She does not give you information, which is the raw material of culture, – she gives you sympathy, which is its subtlest essence.

A more numerous class of silly novels than the oracular, (which are generally inspired by some form of High Church, or transcendental Christianity,) is what we may call the *white neck-cloth* species, which represent the tone of thought and feeling in the Evangelical party. This species is a kind of genteel tract on a large scale, intended as a sort of medicinal sweetmeat for Low Church young ladies; an Evangelical substitute for the fashionable novel, as the May Meetings are a substitute for the Opera. Even Quaker children, one would think, can hardly have been denied the indulgence of a doll; but it must be a doll dressed in a drab gown and a coal-scuttle bonnet – not a worldly doll, in gauze and spangles. And there are no young ladies, we imagine, – unless they belong to the Church of the United Brethren, in which people are married without any love-making – who can dispense with love stories. Thus, for Evangelical young ladies there are Evangelical love stories, in which the vicissitudes of the tender passion are sanctified by saving views of Regeneration and the Atonement. These novels differ from the oracular ones, as a Low Churchwoman often differs from a High Churchwoman: they are a little less supercilious, and a great deal more ignorant, a little less correct in their syntax, and a great deal more vulgar.

The Orlando of Evangelical literature is the young curate, looked at from the point of view of the middle class, where cambric bands are understood to have as thrilling an effect on the hearts of young ladies as epaulettes have in the classes above and below it. In the ordinary type of these novels, the hero is almost sure to be a young curate, frowned upon, perhaps, by worldly mammas, but carrying captive the hearts of their daughters, who can 'never forget *that* sermon'; tender glances are seized from the pulpit stairs instead of the opera-box; *tête-à-têtes* are seasoned with quotations from Scripture, instead of quotations from the poets; and questions as to the state of the heroine's affections are mingled with anxieties as to the state of her soul. The young curate always has a background of well-dressed and wealthy, if not fashionable society; – for Evangelical silliness is as snobbish as any other kind of silliness; and the Evangelical lady novelist, while she explains to you the type of the scapegoat on one page, is ambitious on another to represent the manners and conversation of aristocratic people. Her pictures of fashionable society are often curious studies considered as efforts of the Evangelical imagination; but in one particular the novels of the White Neckcloth School are meritoriously realistic, – their favourite hero, the Evangelical young curate, is always rather an insipid personage.

The most recent novel of this species that we happen to have before us, is *The Old Grey Church*. It is utterly tame and feeble; there is no one set of objects on which the writer seems to have a stronger grasp than on any other; and we should be entirely at a loss to conjecture among what phases of life her experience has been gained, but for certain vulgarisms of style which sufficiently indicate that she has had the advantage, though she has been unable to use it, of mingling chiefly with men and women whose manners and characters have not had all their bosses and angles rubbed down by refined conventionalism. It is less excusable in an Evangelical novelist, than in any other, gratuitously to seek her subjects among titles and carriages. The real drama of Evangelicalism – and it has abundance of fine drama for any one who has genius enough to discern and reproduce it – lies among the middle and lower classes; and are not Evangelical opinions understood to give an especial interest in the weak things of the earth, rather than in the mighty? Why then, cannot our Evangelical lady novelists show us the operation of their religious views among people (there really are many such in the world) who keep no carriage, 'not so much as a brass-bound gig', who even manage to eat their dinner without a silver fork, and in whose mouths the authoress's questionable English would be strictly consistent? Why can we not have pictures of religious life among the industrial classes in England, as interesting as Mrs Stowe's pictures of religious life among the negroes? Instead of this, pious ladies nauseate us with novels which remind us of what we sometimes see in a worldly woman recently 'converted'; – she is as fond of a fine dinner table as before, but she invites clergymen instead of beaux; she thinks as much of her dress as before, but she adopts a more sober choice of colours and patterns; her conversation is as trivial as before, but the triviality is flavoured with Gospel instead of gossip. In *The Old Grey Church*, we have the same sort of Evangelical travesty of the fashionable novel, and of course the vicious, intriguing baronet is not wanting. It is worth while to give a sample of the style of conversation attributed to this high-born rake – a style that in its profuse italics and palpable innuendoes, is worthy of Miss Squeers. In an evening visit to the ruins of the Colosseum, Eustace, the young clergyman, has been withdrawing the heroine, Miss Lushington, from the rest of the party, for the sake of a *tête-à-tête*. The baronet is jealous, and vents his pique in this way: –

There they are, and Miss Lushington, no doubt, quite safe; for she is under the holy guidance of Pope Eustace the First, who has, of course, been delivering to her an edifying homily on the wickedness of the heathens of yore, who, as tradition tells us, in this very place let loose the wild *beasties* on poor Saint Paul! – Oh, no! by the bye, I believe I am wrong, and betraying my want of clergy, and that it was not at all Saint Paul, nor was it here. But no matter, it would equally serve as a text to preach from, and from which to diverge to the degenerate *heathen* Christians of the present day, and all their naughty practices, and so end with an exhortation to 'come out from among them, and be separate'; – and I am sure, Miss Lushington, you have most scrupulously conformed to that injunction this evening, for we have seen nothing of you since our arrival. But every one seems agreed it has been a *charming party of pleasure*, and I am sure we all feel *much indebted* to Mr Grey for having

suggested it; and as he seems so capital a cicerone, I hope
he will think of something else equally agreeable to *all*.

This drivelling kind of dialogue, and equally drivelling
narrative, which, like a bad drawing, represents nothing,
and barely indicates what is meant to be represented,
runs through the book; and we have no doubt is considered by the amiable authoress to constitute an improving
novel, which Christian mothers will do well to put into
the hands of their daughters. But everything is relative;
we have met with American vegetarians whose normal
diet was dry meal, and who, when their appetite wanted
stimulating, tickled it with *wet* meal; and so, we can imagine that there are Evangelical circles in which *The Old
Grey Church* is devoured as a powerful and interesting
fiction.

But, perhaps, the least readable of silly women's novels, are the *modern-antique* species, which unfold to us
the domestic life of Jannes and Jambres, the private love
affairs of Sennacherib, or the mental struggles and ultim-
ate conversion of Demetrius the silversmith. From most
silly novels we can at least extract a laugh; but those of
the modern-antique school have a ponderous, a leaden
kind of fatuity, under which we groan. What can be more
demonstrative of the inability of literary women to
measure their own powers, than their frequent assump-
tion of a task which can only be justified by the rarest
concurrence of acquirement with genius? The finest effort
to reanimate the past is of course only approximative – is
always more or less an infusion of the modern spirit into
the ancient form, –

Was ihr den Geist der Zeiten heisst,
Das ist im Grund der Herren eigner Geist,
In dem die Zeiten sich bespiegeln.

Admitting that genius which has familiarized itself
with all the relics of an ancient period can sometimes, by
the force of its sympathetic divination, restore the missing
notes in the 'music of humanity', and reconstruct the frag-
ments into a whole which will really bring the remote past
nearer to us, and interpret it to our duller apprehension, –
this form of imaginative power must always be among
the very rarest, because it demands as much accurate and
minute knowledge as creative vigour. Yet we find ladies
constantly choosing to make their mental mediocrity
more conspicuous, by clothing it in a masquerade of
ancient names; by putting their feeble sentimentality into
the mouths of Roman vestals or Egyptian princesses, and
attributing their rhetorical arguments to Jewish high-
priests and Greek philosophers. A recent example of this
heavy imbecility is *Adonijah, a Tale of the Jewish Dispersion*, which forms part of a series, 'uniting,' we are told,
'taste, humour, and sound principles'. *Adonijah*, we presume, exemplifies the tale of 'sound principles'; the taste
and humour are to be found in other members of the
series. We are told on the cover, that the incidents of this
tale are 'fraught with unusual interest', and the preface
winds up thus: 'To those who feel interested in the dispersed of Israel and Judea, these pages may afford, perhaps,
information on an important subject, as well as amusement'. Since the 'important subject' on which this book
is to afford information is not specified, it may possibly lie

in some esoteric meaning to which we have no key; but if it has relation to the dispersed of Israel and Judea at any period of their history, we believe a tolerably well-informed school-girl already knows much more of it than she will find in this 'Tale of the Jewish Dispersion'. *Adonijah* is simply the feeblest kind of love story, supposed to be instructive, we presume, because the hero is a Jewish captive, and the heroine a Roman vestal; because they and their friends are converted to Christianity after the shortest and easiest method approved by the 'Society for Promoting the Conversion of the Jews'; and because, instead of being written in plain language, it is adorned with that peculiar style of grandiloquence which is held by some lady novelists to give an antique colouring; and which we recognize at once in such phrases as these: – 'the splendid regnal talents undoubtedly possessed by the Emperor Nero' – 'the expiring scion of a lofty stem' – 'the virtuous partner of his couch' – 'ah, by Vesta!' – and 'I tell thee, Roman'. Among the quotations which serve at once for instruction and ornament on the cover of this volume, there is one from Miss Sinclair, which informs us that 'Works of imagination are *avowedly* read by men of science, wisdom, and piety'; from which we suppose the reader is to gather the cheering inference that Dr Daubeny, Mr Mill, or Mr Maurice, may openly indulge himself with the perusal of *Adonijah*, without being obliged to secrete it among the sofa cushions, or read it by snatches under the dinner-table.

'Be not a baker if your head be made of butter,' says a homely proverb, which, being interpreted, may mean, let no woman rush into print who is not prepared for the consequences. We are aware that our remarks are in a very different tone from that of the reviewers who, with a perennial recurrence of precisely similar emotions, only paralleled, we imagine, in the experience of monthly nurses, tell one lady novelist after another that they 'hail' her productions 'with delight'. We are aware that the ladies at whom our criticism is pointed are accustomed to be told, in the choicest phraseology of puffery, that their pictures of life are brilliant, their characters well-drawn, their style fascinating, and their sentiments lofty. But if they are inclined to resent our plainness of speech, we ask them to reflect for a moment on the chary praise, and often captious blame, which their panegyrists give to writers whose works are on the way to become classics. No sooner does a woman show that she has genius or effective talent, than she receives the tribute of being moderately praised and severely criticized. By a peculiar thermometric adjustment, when a woman's talent is at zero, journalistic approbation is at the boiling pitch; when she attains mediocrity, it is already at no more than summer heat; and if ever she reaches excellence, critical enthusiasm drops to the freezing point. Harriet Martineau, Currer Bell, and Mrs Gaskell have been treated as cavalierly as if they had been men. And every critic who forms a high estimate of the share women may ultimately take in literature, will, on principle, abstain from any exceptional indulgence towards the productions of literary women. For it must be plain to every one who looks impartially and extensively into feminine literature, that its greatest deficiencies are due hardly more to the want of intellectual power than to the want of those moral qualities that contribute to literary excellence – patient diligence, a sense of the responsibility involved in publication, and an appreciation of the sacredness of the writer's art. In the majority of women's books you see that kind of facility which springs from the absence of any high standard; that fertility in imbecile combination or feeble imitation which a little self-criticism would check and reduce to barrenness; just as with a total want of musical ear people will sing out of tune, while a degree more melodic sensibility would suffice to render them silent. The foolish vanity of wishing to appear in print, instead of being counterbalanced by any consciousness of the intellectual or moral derogation implied in futile authorship, seems to be encouraged by the extremely false impression that to write *at all* is a proof of superiority in a woman. On this ground, we believe that the average intellect of women is unfairly represented by the mass of feminine literature, and that while the few women who write well are very far above the ordinary intellectual level of their sex, the many women who write ill are very far below it. So that, after all, the severer critics are fulfilling a chivalrous duty in depriving the mere fact of feminine authorship of any false prestige which may give it a delusive attraction, and in recommending women of mediocre faculties – as at least a negative service they can render their sex – to abstain from writing.

The standing apology for women who become writers without any special qualification is, that society shuts them out from other spheres of occupation. Society is a very culpable entity, and has to answer for the manufacture of many unwholesome commodities, from bad pickles to bad poetry. But society, like 'matter', and Her Majesty's Government, and other lofty abstractions, has its share of excessive blame as well as excessive praise. Where there is one woman who writes from necessity, we believe there are three women who write from vanity; and, besides, there is something so antiseptic in the mere healthy fact of working for one's bread, that the most trashy and rotten kind of feminine literature is not likely to have been produced under such circumstances. 'In all labour there is profit'; but ladies' silly novels, we imagine, are less the result of labour than of busy idleness.

Happily, we are not dependent on argument to prove that Fiction is a department of literature in which women can, after their kind, fully equal men. A cluster of great names, both living and dead, rush to our memories in evidence that women can produce novels not only fine, but among the very finest; – novels, too, that have a precious speciality, lying quite apart from masculine aptitudes and experience. No educational restrictions can shut women out from the materials of fiction, and there is no species of art which is so free from rigid requirements. Like crystalline masses, it may take any form, and yet be beautiful; we have only to pour in the right elements – genuine observation, humour, and passion. But it is precisely this absence of rigid requirement which constitutes the fatal seduction of novel-writing to incompetent women. Ladies are not wont to be very grossly deceived as to their power of playing on the piano; here certain positive difficulties of execution have to be conquered, and incompetence inevitably breaks down. Every art which has its absolute *technique* is, to a certain extent, guarded from the intrusions of mere left-handed imbecility. But in novel-writing there are no barriers for incapacity to stumble against, no external criteria to prevent a writer from mistaking foolish facility for mastery. And so we have again and again the old story of La Fontaine's ass, who puts his nose to the flute, and, finding that he elicits some sound, exclaims, 'Moi, aussi, je joue de la flute'; – a fable which we commend, at parting, to the consideration of any feminine reader who is in danger of adding to the number of 'silly novels by lady novelists'.

Woman in France: Madame de Sablé

In 1847, a certain Count Leopold Ferri died at Padua, leaving a library entirely composed of works written by women, in various languages, and this library amounted to nearly 32,000 volumes. We will not hazard any conjecture as to the proportion of these volumes which a severe judge, like the priest in Don Quixote, would deliver to the flames, but for our own part, most of those we should care to rescue would be the works of French women. With a few remarkable exceptions, our own feminine literature is made up of books which could have been better written by men; books which have the same relation to literature in general, as academic prize poems have to poetry: when not a feeble imitation, they are usually an absurd exaggeration of the masculine style, like the swaggering gait of a bad actress in male attire. Few English women have written so much like a woman as Richardson's Lady C. Now, we think it an immense mistake to maintain that there is no sex in literature. Science has no sex: the mere knowing and reasoning faculties, if they act correctly, must go through the same process, and arrive at the same result. But in art and literature, which imply the action of the entire being, in which every fibre of the nature is engaged, in which every peculiar modification of the individual makes itself felt, woman has something specific to contribute. Under every imaginable social condition, she

will necessarily have a class of sensations and emotions –
the maternal ones – which must remain unknown to man;
and the fact of her comparative physical weakness, which,
however it may have been exaggerated by a vicious civilization, can never be cancelled, introduces a distinctively
feminine condition into the wondrous chemistry of the
affections and sentiments, which inevitably gives rise to
distinctive forms and combinations. A certain amount of
psychological difference between man and woman necessarily arises out of the difference of sex, and instead of
being destined to vanish before a complete development
of woman's intellectual and moral nature, will be a permanent source of variety and beauty, as long as the tender
light and dewy freshness of morning affect us differently
from the strength and brilliancy of the mid-day sun. And
those delightful women of France, who, from the beginning of the seventeenth to the close of the eighteenth century, formed some of the brightest threads in the web of
political and literary history, wrote under circumstances
which left the feminine character of their minds uncramped
by timidity, and unstrained by mistaken effort. They were
not trying to make a career for themselves; they thought
little, in many cases not at all, of the public; they wrote
letters to their lovers and friends, memoirs of their every-
day lives, romances in which they gave portraits of their
familiar acquaintances, and described the tragedy or com-
edy which was going on before their eyes. Always refined
and graceful, often witty, sometimes judicious, they wrote
what they saw, thought, and felt, in their habitual language, without proposing any model to themselves, without any intention to prove that women could write as well

as men, without affecting manly views or suppressing womanly ones. One may say, at least with regard to the women of the seventeenth century, that their writings were but a charming accident of their more charming lives, like the petals which the wind shakes from the rose in its bloom. And it is but a twin fact with this, that in France alone woman has had a vital influence on the development of literature; in France alone the mind of woman has passed like an electric current through the language, making crisp and definite what is elsewhere heavy and blurred; in France alone, if the writings of women were swept away, a serious gap would be made in the national history.

Patriotic gallantry may perhaps contend that English women could, if they had liked, have written as well as their neighbours; but we will leave the consideration of that question to the reviewers of the literature that might have been. In the literature that actually is, we must turn to France for the highest examples of womanly achievement in almost every department. We confess ourselves unacquainted with the productions of those awful women of Italy, who held professional chairs, and were great in civil and canon law; we have made no researches into the catacombs of female literature, but we think we may safely conclude that they would yield no rivals to that which is still unburied; and here, we suppose, the question of preeminence can only lie between England and France. And to this day, Madame de Sévigné remains the single instance of a woman who is supreme in a class of literature which has engaged the ambition of men; Madame Dacier still reigns the queen of blue-stockings, though women have long studied Greek without shame;* Madame de Staël's name still rises first to the lips when we are asked to mention a woman of great intellectual power; Madame Roland is still the unrivalled type of the sagacious and sternly heroic, yet lovable woman; George Sand is the unapproached artist who, to Jean-Jacques' eloquence and deep sense of external nature, unites the clear delineation of character and the tragic depth of passion. These great names, which mark different epochs, soar like tall pines amidst a forest of less conspicuous, but not less fascinating, female writers; and beneath these again are spread, like a thicket of hawthorns, eglantines, and honeysuckles, the women who are known rather by what they stimulated men to write, than by what they wrote themselves – the women whose tact, wit, and personal radiance, created the atmosphere of the *salon*, where literature, philosophy, and science, emancipated from the trammels of pedantry and technicality, entered on a brighter stage of existence.

What were the causes of this earlier development and more abundant manifestation of womanly intellect in France? The primary one, perhaps, lies in the physiological characteristics of the Gallic race: – the small brain and vivacious temperament which permit the fragile system

* Queen Christina, when Madame Dacier (then Mademoiselle Le Fèvre) sent her a copy of her edition of *Callimachus*, wrote in reply; – 'Mais vous, de qui on m'assure que vous êtes une belle et agréable fille, n'avez vous pas honte de'être si savante?' [The sentence translates as 'But you, a handsome and pleasing maid, as I am told, are you not ashamed of being so learned?']

of woman to sustain the superlative activity requisite for intellectual creativeness; while, on the other hand, the larger brain and slower temperament of the English and Germans are, in the womanly organization, generally dreamy and passive. The type of humanity in the latter may be grander, but it requires a larger sum of conditions to produce a perfect specimen. Throughout the animal world, the higher the organization, the more frequent is the departure from the normal form; we do not often see imperfectly-developed or ill-made insects, but we rarely see a perfectly-developed, well-made man. And thus the *physique* of a woman may suffice as the substratum for a superior Gallic mind, but is too thin a soil for a superior Teutonic one. Our theory is borne out by the fact, that among our own countrywomen, those who distinguish themselves by literary production, more frequently approach the Gallic than the Teutonic type; they are intense and rapid rather than comprehensive. The woman of large capacity can seldom rise beyond the absorption of ideas; her physical conditions refuse to support the energy required for spontaneous activity; the voltaic-pile is not strong enough to produce crystallizations; phantasms of great ideas float through her mind, but she has not the spell which will arrest them, and give them fixity. This, more than unfavourable external circumstances, is, we think, the reason why woman has not yet contributed any new form to art, any discovery in science, any deep-searching inquiry in philosophy. The necessary physiological conditions are not present in her. That under more favourable circumstances in the future, these conditions may prove compatible with the feminine organization, it would be rash to deny. For the present, we are only concerned with our theory so far as it presents a physiological basis for the intellectual effectiveness of French women.

A secondary cause was probably the laxity of opinion and practice with regard to the marriage-tie. Heaven forbid that we should enter on a defence of French morals, most of all in relation to marriage! But it is undeniable, that unions formed in the maturity of thought and feeling, and grounded only on inherent fitness and mutual attraction, tended to bring women into more intelligent sympathy with men, and to heighten and complicate their share in the political drama. The quiescence and security of the conjugal relation, are doubtless favourable to the manifestation of the highest qualities by persons who have already attained a high standard of culture, but rarely foster a passion sufficient to rouse all the faculties to aid in winning or retaining its beloved object – to convert indolence into activity, indifference into ardent partisanship, dullness into perspicuity. Gallantry and intrigue are sorry enough things in themselves, but they certainly serve better to arouse the dormant faculties of woman than embroidery and domestic drudgery, especially when, as in the high society of France in the seventeenth century, they are refined by the influence of Spanish chivalry, and controlled by the spirit of Italian causticity. The dreamy and fantastic girl was awakened to reality by the experience of wifehood and maternity, and became capable of loving, not a mere phantom of her own imagination, but a living man, struggling with the hatreds and rivalries of the political arena; she espoused his quarrels, she made herself, her fortune, and her influence, the stepping-stones of his ambition; and the languid beauty, who had formerly seemed ready to 'die of a rose', was seen to become the heroine of an insurrection. The vivid interest in affairs which was thus excited in woman, must obviously have tended to quicken her intellect, and give it a practical application; and the very sorrows – the heart-pangs and regrets which are inseparable from a life of passion – deepened her nature by the questioning of self and destiny which they occasioned, and by the energy demanded to surmount them and live on. No wise person, we imagine, wishes to restore the social condition of France in the seventeenth century, or considers the ideal programme of woman's life to be a *mariage de convenance* at fifteen, a career of gallantry from twenty to eight-and-thirty, and penitence and piety for the rest of her days. Nevertheless, that social condition had its good results, as much as the madly-superstitious Crusades had theirs.

But the most indisputable source of feminine culture and development in France was the influence of the *salons*; which, as all the world knows, were *réunions* of both sexes, where conversation ran along the whole gamut of subjects, from the frothiest *vers de société* to the philosophy of Descartes. Richelieu had set the fashion of uniting a taste for letters with the habits of polite society and the pursuits of ambition; and in the first quarter of the seventeenth century, there were already several *hôtels* in Paris, varying in social position from the closest proximity of the Court to the debatable ground of the aristocracy and the bourgeoisie, which served as a rendezvous for different circles of people, bent on entertaining themselves either by showing talent or admiring it. The most

celebrated of these rendezvous was the Hôtel de Rambouillet, which was at the culmination of its glory in
1630, and did not become quite extinct until 1648, when,
the troubles of the Fronde commencing, its *habitués* were
dispersed or absorbed by political interests. The presiding
genius of this *salon*, the Marquise de Rambouillet, was
the very model of the woman who can act as an amalgam
to the most incongruous elements; beautiful, but not pre-
occupied by coquetry or passion; an enthusiastic admirer
of talent, but with no pretensions to talent on her own
part; exquisitely refined in language and manners, but
warm and generous withal; not given to entertain her
guests with her own compositions, or to paralyse them
by her universal knowledge. She had once *meant* to learn
Latin, but had been prevented by an illness; perhaps she
was all the better acquainted with Italian and Spanish
productions, which, in default of a national literature,
were then the intellectual pabulum of all cultivated persons in France who were unable to read the classics. In her
mild, agreeable presence was accomplished that blending
of the high-toned chivalry of Spain with the caustic wit
and refined irony of Italy, which issued in the creation of
a new standard of taste – the combination of the utmost
exaltation in sentiment with the utmost simplicity of
language. Women are peculiarly fitted to further such a
combination, – first, from their greater tendency to mingle
affection and imagination with passion, and thus subti-
lize it into sentiment; and next, from that dread of what
over-taxes their intellectual energies, either by difficulty
or monotony, which gives them an instinctive fondness
for lightness of treatment and airiness of expression, thus

making them cut short all prolixity and reject all heaviness. When these womanly characteristics were brought into conversational contact with the materials furnished by such minds as those of Richelieu, Corneille, the Great Condé, Balzac, and Bossuet, it is no wonder that the result was something piquant and charming. Those famous *habitués* of the Hôtel de Rambouillet did not, apparently, first lay themselves out to entertain the ladies with grimacing 'small-talk', and then take each other by the sword-knot to discuss matters of real interest in a corner; they rather sought to present their best ideas in the guise most acceptable to intelligent and accomplished women. And the conversation was not of literature only; war, politics, religion, the lightest details of daily news – everything was admissible, if only it were treated with refinement and intelligence. The Hôtel de Rambouillet was no mere literary *réunion*; it included *hommes d'affaires* and soldiers as well as authors, and in such a circle, women would not become *bas bleus* or dreamy moralizers, ignorant of the world and of human nature, but intelligent observers of character and events. It is easy to understand, however, that with the herd of imitators who, in Paris and the provinces, aped the style of this famous *salon*, simplicity degenerated into affectation, and nobility of sentiment was replaced by an inflated effort to outstrip nature, so that the *genre précieux* drew down the satire, which reached its climax in the *Précieuses ridicules* and *Les Femmes savantes*, the former of which appeared in 1660, and the latter in 1673. But Madelon and Cathos are the lineal descendants of Mademoiselle Scudéry and her satellites quite as much as of the Hôtel de Rambouillet. The society which assembled every Saturday in her *salon* was exclusively literary, and, although occasionally visited by a few persons of high birth, bourgeois in its tone, and enamoured of madrigals, sonnets, stanzas, and *bouts rimés*. The affectation that decks trivial things in fine language, belongs essentially to a class which sees another above it, and is uneasy in the sense of its inferiority; and this affectation is precisely the opposite of the original *genre précieux*.

Another centre from which feminine influence radiated into the national literature was the Palais du Luxembourg, where Mademoiselle d'Orléans, in disgrace at court on account of her share in the Fronde, held a little court of her own, and for want of anything else to employ her active spirit, busied herself with literature. One fine morning, it occurred to this princess to ask all the persons who frequented her court, among whom were Madame de Sévigné, Madame de la Fayette, and La Rochefoucauld, to write their own portraits, and she at once set the example. It was understood that defects and virtues were to be spoken of with like candour. The idea was carried out; those who were not clever or not bold enough to write for themselves employing the pen of a friend.

'Such,' says M. Cousin, 'was the pastime of Mademoiselle and her friends during the years 1657 and 1658: from this pastime proceeded a complete literature. In 1659, Ségrais revised these portraits, added a considerable number in prose and even in verse, and published the whole in a handsome quarto volume, admirably printed, and now become very rare, under the title, *Divers Portraits*. Only thirty copies were printed, not for sale, but to be given as presents by Mademoiselle. The work had a prodigious success. That which had made the fortune of Mademoiselle de Scudéry's romances – the pleasure of seeing one's portrait a little flattered, curiosity to see that of others, the passion which the middle class always have had an d will have for knowing what goes on in the aristocratic world (at that time not very easy of access), the names of the illustrious persons who were here for the first time described physically and morally with the utmost detail, great ladies transformed all at once into writers, and unconsciously inventing a new manner of writing, of which no book gave the slightest idea, and which was the ordinary manner of speaking of the aristocracy; this undefinable mixture of the natural, the easy, and at the same time of the agreeable, and supremely distinguished – all this charmed the court and the town, and very early in the year 1659 permission was asked of Mademoiselle to give a new edition of the privileged book for the use of the public in general.

The fashion thus set, portraits multiplied throughout France, until in 1688, La Bruyère adopted the form in his *Characters*, and ennobled it by divesting it of personality. We shall presently see that a still greater work than La Bruyère's also owed its suggestion to a woman, whose *salon* was hardly a less fascinating resort than the Hôtel de Rambouillet itself.

In proportion as the literature of a country is enriched and culture becomes more generally diffused, personal influence is less effective in the formation of taste and in the furtherance of social advancement. It is no longer the coterie which acts on literature, but literature which acts on the coterie; the circle represented by the word *public*, is ever widening, and ambition, poising itself in order to hit a more distant mark, neglects the successes of the *salon*. What was once lavished prodigally in conversation, is reserved for the volume, or the 'article'; and the effort is not to betray originality rather than to communicate it. As the old coach-roads have sunk into disuse through the creation of railways, so journalism tends more and more to divert information from the channel of conversation into the channel of the Press: no one is satisfied with a more circumscribed audience than that very indeterminate abstraction 'the public', and men find a vent for their opinions not in talk, but in 'copy'. We read the *Athenæum* askance at the tea-table, and take notes from the *Philosophical Journal* at a soirée; we invite our friends that we may thrust a book into their hands, and presuppose an exclusive desire in the 'ladies' to discuss their own matters, 'that we may crackle the *Times*' at our ease. In fact, the evident tendency of things to contract personal communication within the narrowest limits makes us tremble lest some further development of the electric telegraph should reduce us to a society of mutes, or to a sort of insect, communicating by ingenious antennæ of our own invention. Things were far from having reached this pass in the last century; but even then, literature and society had outgrown the nursing of coteries, and although many *salons* of that period were worthy successors of the Hôtel de Rambouillet, they were simply a recreation, not an influence. Enviable evenings, no doubt, were passed in them; and if we could be carried back to any of them at will, we should hardly know whether to choose the Wednesday dinner at Madame Geoffrin's, with d'Alembert, Mademoiselle de l'Espinasse, Grimm, and the rest, or the graver society which, thirty years later, gathered round Condorcet and his lovely young wife. The *salon* retained its attractions, but its power was gone: the stream of life had become too broad and deep for such small rills to affect it.

A fair comparison between the French women of the seventeenth century and those of the eighteenth would, perhaps, have a balanced result, though it is common to be a partisan on this subject. The former have more exaltation, perhaps more nobility of sentiment, and less consciousness in their intellectual activity – less of the *femme auteur*, which was Rousseau's horror in Madame d'Epinay, but the latter have a richer fund of ideas – not more ingenuity, but the materials of an additional century for their ingenuity to work upon. The women of the seventeenth century, when love was on the wane, took to devotion, at first mildly and by halves, as English women take to caps, and finally without compromise; with the women of the eighteenth century, Bossuet and Massillon had given way to Voltaire and Rousseau; and when youth and beauty failed, then they were thrown on their own moral strength.

M. Cousin is especially enamoured of the women of the seventeenth century, and relieves himself from his labours in philosophy by making researches into the original documents which throw light upon their lives. Last year he gave us some results of these researches, in a volume on the youth of the Duchesse de Longueville, and he has just followed it up with a second volume, in which he further illustrates her career by tracing it in connexion with that of her friend, Madame de Sablé. The materials to which he has had recourse for this purpose, are chiefly two celebrated collections of manuscripts: that of Conrart, the first secretary to the French Academy, one of those universally curious people who seem made for the annoyance of contemporaries and the benefit of posterity; and that of Valant, who was at once the physician, the secretary, and general steward of Madame de Sablé, and who, with or without her permission, possessed himself of the letters addressed to her by her numerous correspondents during the latter part of her life, and of various papers having some personal or literary interest attached to them. From these stores M. Cousin has selected many documents previously unedited; and though he often leaves us something to desire in the arrangement of his materials, this volume of his on Madame de Sablé is very acceptable to us, for she interests us quite enough to carry us through more than three hundred pages of rather scattered narrative, and through an appendix of correspondence in small type. M. Cousin justly appreciates her character as 'un heureux mélange de raison, d'esprit, d'agrément, et de bonté'; and perhaps there are few better specimens of the woman who is extreme in nothing, but sympathetic in all things; who affects us by no special quality, but by her entire being; whose nature has no *tons criards*, but is like those textures which, from their harmonious blending of all colours, give repose to the eye, and do not weary us though we see them every day. Madame de Sablé is also a striking example of the one order of influence which woman has exercised over literature in France; and on this ground, as well as intrinsically, she is worth studying. If the reader agrees with us he will perhaps be inclined, as we are, to dwell a little on the chief points in her life and character.

Madeline de Souvré, daughter of the Marquis of Courtenvaux, a nobleman distinguished enough to be chosen as governor of Louis XIII, was born in 1599, on the threshold of that seventeenth century, the brilliant genius of which is mildly reflected in her mind and history. Thus, when in 1635 her more celebrated friend, Mademoiselle de Bourbon, afterwards the Duchesse de Longueville, made her appearance at the Hôtel de Rambouillet, Madame de Sablé had nearly crossed that table-land of maturity which precedes a woman's descent towards old age. She had been married, in 1614, to Philippe Emanuel de Laval-Montmorency, Seigneur de Bois-Dauphin, and Marquis de Sablé, of whom nothing further is known than that he died in 1640, leaving her the richer by four children, but with a fortune considerably embarrassed. With beauty and high rank added to the mental attractions of which we have abundant evidence, we may well believe that Madame de Sablé's youth was brilliant. For her beauty, we have the testimony of sober Madame de Motteville, who also speaks of her as having 'beaucoup de lumière et de sincérité'; and in the following passage very graphically indicates one phase of Madame de Sablé's character: –

The Marquise de Sablé was one of those whose beauty made the most noise when the Queen came into France.

But if she was amiable, she was still more desirous of appearing so; this lady's self-love rendered her too sensitive to the regard which men exhibited towards her. There yet existed in France some remains of the politeness which Catherine de Médici had introduced from Italy, and the new dramas, with all the other works in prose and verse, which came from Madrid, were thought to have such great delicacy, that she (Madame de Sablé) had conceived a high idea of the gallantry which the Spaniards had learned from the Moors.

She was persuaded that men can, without crime, have tender sentiments for women – that the desire of pleasing them led men to the greatest and finest actions – roused their intelligence, and inspired them with liberality, and all sorts of virtues; but, on the other hand, women, who were the ornament of the world, and made to be served and adored, ought not to admit anything from them but their respectful attentions. As this lady supported her views with much talent and great beauty, she had given them authority in her time, and the number and consideration of those who continued to associate with her, have caused to subsist in our day what the Spaniards call *finezas*.

Here is the grand element of the original *femme précieuse*, and it appears further, in a detail also reported by Madame de Motteville, that Madame de Sablé had a passionate admirer in the accomplished Duc de Montmorency, and apparently reciprocated his regard; but discovering (at what period of their attachment is unknown) that he was raising a lover's eyes towards the Queen, she broke with him at once. 'I have heard her say,' tells Madame de Motteville, 'that her pride was such with regard to the Duc de Montmorency, that at the first demonstrations which he gave of his change, she refused to see him any more, being unable to receive with satisfaction attentions which she had to share with the greatest princess in the world.' There is no evidence, except the untrustworthy assertion of Tallemant de Réaux, that Madame de Sablé had any other liaison than this; and the probability of the negative is increased by the ardour of her friendships. The strongest of these was formed early in life with Mademoiselle Dona d'Attichy, afterwards Comtesse de Maure; it survived the effervescence of youth and the closest intimacy of middle age, and was only terminated by the death of the latter in 1663. A little incident in this friendship is so characteristic in the transcendentalism which was then carried into all the affections, that it is worth relating at length. Mademoiselle d'Attichy, in her grief and indignation at Richelieu's treatment of her relative, quitted Paris, and was about to join her friend at Sablé, when she suddenly discovered that Madame de Sablé, in a letter to Madame de Rambouillet, had said, that her greatest happiness would be to pass her life with Julie de Rambouillet, afterwards Madame de Montausier. To Anne d'Attichy this appears nothing less than the crime of *lèse-amitié*. No explanations will appease her: she refuses to accept the assurance that the offensive expression was used simply out of unreflecting conformity to the style of the Hôtel de Rambouillet – that it was mere '*galimatias*'. She gives up her journey, and writes a letter, which is the only one Madame de Sablé chose to preserve, when, in her period of devotion, she sacrificed the records of her youth. Here it is: –

I have seen this letter in which you tell me there is so much *galimatias*, and I assure you that I have not found any at all. On the contrary, I find everything very plainly expressed, and among others, one which is too explicit for my satisfaction – namely, what you have said to Madame de Rambouillet, that if you tried to imagine a perfectly happy life for yourself, it would be to pass it all alone with Mademoiselle de Rambouillet. You know whether any one can be more persuaded than I am of her merit; but I confess to you that that has not prevented me from being surprised that you could entertain a thought which did so great an injury to our friendship. As to believing that you said this to one, and wrote it to the other, simply for the sake of paying them an agreeable compliment, I have too high an esteem for your courage to be able to imagine that complaisance would cause you thus to betray the sentiments of your heart, especially on a subject in which, as they were un-favourable to me, I think you would have the more reason for concealing them, the affection which I have for you being so well-known to every one, and especially to Made-moiselle de Rambouillet, so that I doubt whether she will not have been more sensible of the wrong you have done me, than of the advantage you have given her. The circum-stance of this letter falling into my hands, has forcibly reminded me of these lines of Bertaut: –

> Malheureuse est l'ignorance.
> Et plus malheureux le savoir.

Having through this lost a confidence which alone rendered life supportable to me, it is impossible for me to take the journey so much thought of. For would there be any propriety in travelling sixty miles in this season, in order to burthen you with a person so little suited to you, that after years of a passion without parallel, you cannot help thinking that the greatest pleasure of your life would be to pass it without her? I return, then, into my solitude, to examine the defects which cause me so much unhappiness, and unless I can correct them, I should have less joy than confusion in seeing you.

It speaks strongly for the charm of Madame de Sablé's nature that she was able to retain so susceptible a friend as Mademoiselle d'Attichy in spite of numerous other friendships, some of which, especially that with Madame de Longueville, were far from lukewarm – in spite too of a tendency in herself to distrust the affection of others towards her, and to wait for advances rather than to make them. We find many traces of this tendency in the affectionate remonstrances addressed to her by Madame de Longueville, now for shutting herself up from her friends, now for doubting that her letters are acceptable. Here is a little passage from one of these remonstrances which indicates a trait of Madame de Sablé, and is in itself a bit of excellent sense, worthy the consideration of lovers and friends in general: –

I am very much afraid that if I leave to you the care of letting me know when I can see you, I shall be a long time without having that pleasure, and that nothing will

incline you to procure it me, for I have always observed
a certain lukewarmness in your friendship after our
explanations, from which I have never seen you thoroughly recover; and that is why I dread explanations, for
however good they may be in themselves, since they
serve to reconcile people, it must always be admitted, to
their shame, that they are at least the effect of a bad
cause, and that if they remove it for a time they *sometimes leave a certain facility in getting angry again*, which,
without diminishing friendship, renders its intercourse
less agreeable. It seems to me that I find all this in your
behaviour to me; so I am not wrong in sending to know
if you wish to have me to-day.

It is clear that Madame de Sablé was far from having
what Sainte-Beuve calls the one fault of Madame Necker –
absolute perfection. A certain exquisiteness in her physical and moral nature was, as we shall see, the source of
more than one weakness, but the perception of these weaknesses, which is indicated in Madame de Longueville's letters, heightens our idea of the attractive qualities which
notwithstanding drew from her, at the sober age of forty,
such expressions as these: – 'I assure you that you are the
person in all the world whom it would be most agreeable
to me to see, and there is no one whose intercourse is a
ground of truer satisfaction to me. It is admirable that at
all times, and amidst all changes, the taste for your society
remains in me; and, *if one ought to thank God for the joys
which do not tend to salvation*, I should thank him with all
my heart for having preserved that to me at a time in
which he has taken away from me all others.'

Since we have entered on the chapter of Madame de Sablé's weaknesses, this is the place to mention what was the subject of endless raillery from her friends – her elaborate precaution about her health, and her dread of infection, even from diseases the least communicable. Perhaps this anxiety was founded as much on aesthetic as on physical grounds, on disgust at the details of illness as much as on dread of suffering: with a cold in the head or a bilious complaint, the exquisite *précieuse* must have been considerably less conscious of being 'the ornament of the world', and 'made to be adored'. Even her friendship, strong as it was, was not strong enough to overcome her horror of contagion; for when Mademoiselle de Bourbon, recently become Madame de Longueville, was attacked by small-pox, Madame de Sablé for some time had not courage to visit her, or even to see Mademoiselle de Rambouillet, who was assiduous in her attendance on the patient. A little correspondence *à propos* of these circumstances so well exhibits the graceful badinage in which the great ladies of that day were adepts, that we are tempted to quote one short letter.

Mademoiselle de Rambouillet to the Marquise de Sablé

Mademoiselle de Chalais (*dame de compagnie* to the Marquise) will please to read this letter to Madame la Marquise, *out of* a draught.

Madame,

I do not think it possible to begin my treaty with you too early, for I am convinced that between the first proposition made to me that I should see you, and the conclusion, you will have so many reflections to make, so many physicians to consult, and so many fears to sur- mount, that I shall have full leisure to air myself. The conditions which I offer to fulfil for this purpose are, not to visit you until I have been three days absent from the Hôtel de Condé (where Madame de Longueville was ill), to choose a frosty day, not to approach you within four paces, not to sit down on more than one seat. You may also have a great fire in your room, burn juniper in the four corners, surround yourself with imperial vinegar, with rue and wormwood. If you can feel yourself safe under these conditions, without my cutting off my hair, I swear to you to execute them religiously; and if you want examples to fortify you, I can tell you that the Queen consented to see M. Chaudebonne, when he had come directly from Mademoiselle de Bourbon's room, and that Madame d'Aiguillon, who has good taste in such matters, and is free from reproach on these points, has just sent me word that if I did not go to see her, she would come to me.

Madame de Sablé betrays in her reply that she winces under this raillery, and thus provokes a rather severe though polite rejoinder, which, added to the fact that Madame de Longueville is convalescent, rouses her cour- age to the pitch of paying the formidable visit. Mademois- elle de Rambouillet, made aware, through their mutual friend Voiture, that her sarcasm has cut rather too deep, winds up the matter by writing that very difficult pro- duction, a perfectly conciliatory yet dignified apology.

Peculiarities like this always deepen with age, and accordingly, fifteen years later, we find Madame d'Orléans, in her *Princesse de Paphlagonia* – a romance in which she describes her court, with the little quarrels and other affairs that agitated it – giving the following amusing picture, or rather caricature, of the extent to which Madame de Sablé carried her pathological mania, which seems to have been shared by her friend the Countess de Maure (Mademoiselle d'Attichy). In the romance, these two ladies appear under the names of the Princesse Parthénie and the Reine de Mionie.

There was not an hour in the day in which they did not confer together on the means of avoiding death, and on the art of rendering themselves immortal. Their conferences did not take place like those of other people; the fear of breathing an air which was too cold or too warm, the dread lest the wind should be too dry or too moist – in short, the imagination that the weather might not be as temperate as they thought necessary for the preservation of their health, caused them to write letters from one room to the other. It would be extremely fortunate if these notes could be found, and formed into a collection. I am convinced that they would contain rules for the regimen of life, precautions even as to the proper time for applying remedies, and also remedies which Hippocrates and Galen, with all their science, never heard of. Such a collection would be very useful to the public, and would be highly profitable to the faculties of Paris and Montpelier. If these letters were discovered, great advantages of all kinds might be derived from them, for they were princesses who had nothing mortal about them but the *knowledge* that they were mortal. In their writings might be learned all politeness in style, and the most delicate manner of speaking on all subjects. There is nothing with which they were not acquainted; they knew the affairs of all the States in the world, through the share they had in all the intrigues of its private members, either in matters of gallantry, as in other things on which their advice was necessary; either to adjust embroilments and quarrels, or to excite them, for the sake of the advantages which their friends could derive from them; – in a word, they were persons through whose hands the secrets of the whole world had to pass. The Princess Parthénie (Madame de Sablé) had a palate as delicate as her mind; nothing could equal the magnificence of the entertainments she gave; all the dishes were exquisite, and her cleanliness was beyond all that could be imagined. It was in their time that writing came into use; previously, nothing was written but marriage contracts, and letters were never heard of; thus it is to them that we owe a practice so convenient in intercourse.

Still later, in 1669, when the most uncompromising of the Port-Royalists seemed to tax Madame de Sablé with lukewarmness that she did not join them at Port-Royal des Champs, we find her writing to the stern M. de Sévigny: 'En vérité, je crois que je ne pourrois mieux faire que de tout quitter et de m'en aller là. Mais que deviendroient ces frayeurs de n'avoir pas de médecins à choisir, ni de chirurgien pour me saigner?'

Mademoiselle, as we have seen, hints at the love of delicate eating, which many of Madame de Sablé's friends numbered among her foibles, especially after her religious career had commenced. She had a genius in *friandise*, and knew how to gratify the palate without offending the highest sense of refinement. Her sympathetic nature showed itself in this as in other things: she was always sending *bonnes bouches* to her friends, and trying to communicate to them her science and taste in the affairs of the table. Madame de Longueville, who had not the luxurious tendencies of her friend, writes – 'Je vous demande au nom de Dieu, que vous ne me prépariez aucun ragoût. Surtout ne me donnez point de festin. Au nom de Dieu, qu'il n'y ait rien que ce qu'on peut manger, car vous savez que c'est inutile pour moi; de plus j'en ai scrupule.' But other friends had more appreciation of her niceties. Voiture thanks her for her melons, and assures her that they are better than those of yesterday; Madame de Choisy hopes that her ridicule of Jansenism will not provoke Madame de Sablé to refuse her the receipt for salad; and La Rochefoucauld writes: 'You cannot do me a greater charity than to permit the bearer of this letter to enter into the mysteries of your marmalade and your genuine preserves, and I humbly entreat you to do everything you can in his favour. If I could hope for two dishes of those preserves, which I did not deserve to eat before, I should be indebted to you all my life.' For our own part, being as far as possible from fraternizing with those spiritual people who convert a deficiency into a principle, and pique themselves on an obtuse palate as a point of superiority, we are not inclined to number Madame de Sablé's *friandise* amongst her defects. M. Cousin, too, is apologetic on this point. He says:

> It was only the excess of a delicacy which can be readily understood, and a sort of fidelity to the character of *précieuse*. As the *précieuse* did nothing according to common usage, she could not dine like another. We have cited a passage from Madame de Motteville, where Madame de Sablé is represented in her first youth at the Hôtel de Rambouillet, maintaining that woman is born to be an ornament to the world, and to receive the adoration of men. The woman worthy of the name, ought always to appear above material wants, and retain, even in the most vulgar details of life, something distinguished and purified. Eating is a very necessary operation, but one which is not agreeable to the eye. Madame de Sablé insisted on its being conducted with a peculiar cleanliness. According to her, it was not every woman who could with impunity be at table in the presence of a lover; the first distortion of the face, she said, would be enough to spoil all. Gross meals, made for the body merely, ought to be abandoned to *bourgeoises*, and the refined woman should appear to take a little nourishment merely to sustain her, and even to divert her, as one takes refreshments and ices. Wealth did not suffice for this; a particular talent was required. Madame de Sablé was a mistress in this art. She had transported the aristocratic spirit and the *genre précieux*, good breeding and good taste, even into cookery. Her dinners, without any opulence, were celebrated and sought after.

It is quite in accordance with all this, that Madame de Sablé should delight in fine scents, and we find that she did; for being threatened, in her Port-Royal days, when she was at an advanced age, with the loss of smell, and writing for sympathy and information to Mère Agnès, who had lost that sense early in life, she receives this admonition from the stern saint: 'You would gain by this loss, my very dear sister, if you made use of it as a satisfaction to God, for having had too much pleasure in delicious scents.' Scarron describes her as

> La non pareille Bois-Dauphine,
> *Entre dames perle très fine,*

and the superlative delicacy implied by this epithet seems to have belonged equally to her personal habits, her affections, and her intellect.

Madame de Sablé's life, for anything we know, flowed on evenly enough until 1640, when the death of her husband threw upon her the care of an embarrassed fortune. She found a friend in René de Longueil, Seigneur de Maisons, of whom we are content to know no more than that he helped Madame de Sablé to arrange her affairs, though only by means of alienating from her family the estate of Sablé, that his house was her refuge during the blockade of Paris, in 1649, and that she was not unmindful of her obligations to him, when, subsequently, her credit could be serviceable to him at court. In the midst of these pecuniary troubles came a more terrible trial – the loss of her favourite son, the brave and handsome Guy de Laval, who, after a brilliant career in the campaigns of

Condé, was killed at the siege of Dunkirk, in 1646, when scarcely four-and-twenty. The fine qualities of this young man had endeared him to the whole army, and especially to Condé, had won him the hand of the Chancellor Séguire's daughter, and had thus opened to him the prospect of the highest honours. His loss seems to have been the most real sorrow of Madame de Sablé's life. Soon after followed the commotions of the Fronde, which put a stop to social intercourse, and threw the closest friends into opposite ranks. According to Lenet, who relies on the authority of Gourville, Madame de Sablé was under strong obligations to the court, being in the receipt of a pension of 2,000 crowns; at all events, she adhered throughout to the Queen and Mazarin, but being as far as possible from a fierce partisan, and given both by disposition and judgement to hear both sides of a question, she acted as a conciliator, and retained her friends of both parties. The Countess de Maure, whose husband was the most obstinate of *frondeurs*, remained throughout her most cherished friend, and she kept up a constant correspondence with the lovely and intrepid heroine of the Fronde, Madame de Longueville. Her activity was directed to the extinction of animosities, by bringing about marriages between the Montagues and Capulets of the Fronde – between the Prince de Condé, or his brother, and the niece of Mazarin, or between the three nieces of Mazarin and the sons of three noblemen who were distinguished leaders of the Fronde. Though her projects were not realized, her conciliatory position enabled her to preserve all her friendships intact, and when the political tempest was over, she could assemble around her in her residence, in the Place Royale, the same society as before. Madame de Sablé was now approaching her twelfth lustrum, and though the charms of her mind and character made her more sought after than most younger women, it is not surprising that, sharing as she did in the religious ideas of her time, the concerns of 'salvation' seemed to become pressing. A religious retirement, which did not exclude the reception of literary friends, or the care for personal comforts, made the most becoming frame for age and diminished fortune. Jansenism was then to ordinary Catholicism what Puseyism is to ordinary Church of Englandism in these days – it was a *recherché* form of piety unshared by the vulgar; and one sees at once that it must have special attractions for the *précieuse*. Madame de Sablé, then, probably about 1655 or 1656, determined to retire to Port-Royal, not because she was already devout, but because she hoped to become so; as, however, she wished to retain the pleasure of intercourse with friends who were still worldly, she built for herself a set of apartments at once distinct from the monastery and attached to it. Here, with a comfortable establishment, consisting of her secretary, Dr Valant, Mademoiselle de Chalais, formerly her *dame de compagnie*, and now become her friend; an excellent cook; a few other servants, and for a considerable time a carriage and coachman; with her best friends within a moderate distance, she could, as M. Cousin says, be out of the noise of the world without altogether forsaking it, preserve her dearest friendships, and have before her eyes edifying examples – 'vaquer enfin à son aise aux soins de son salut et à ceux de sa santé'.

We have hitherto looked only at one phase of Madame

de Sablé's character and influence – that of the *précieuse*.
But she was much more than this: she was the valuable,
trusted friend of noble women and distinguished men;
she was the animating spirit of a society whence issued a
new form of French literature: she was the woman of
large capacity and large heart, whom Pascal sought to
please, to whom Arnauld submitted the Discourse prefixed to his Logic, and to whom La Rochefoucauld writes:
'Vous savez que je ne crois que vous êtes sûr de certains
chapitres, et surtout sur les replis du cœur.' The papers
preserved by her secretary, Valant, show that she maintained an extensive correspondence with persons of various rank and character; that her pen was untiring in the
interest of others; that men made her the depositary of
their thoughts, women of their sorrows; that her friends
were as impatient, when she secluded herself, as if they
had been rival lovers and she a youthful beauty. It is into
her ear that Madame de Longueville pours her troubles
and difficulties, and that Madame de la Fayette commu-
nicates her little alarms, lest young Count de St Paul
should have detected her intimacy with La Rochefoucauld.* The few of Madame de Sablé's letters which

---

* The letter to which we allude has this charming little touch;– 'Je hais
comme la mort que les gens de son age puissent croire que j'ai des
galanteries. Il semble qu'on leur parait cent ans des qu'on est plus
vieille qu' eux, et ils sont tout propre à s'étonner qu'il y ait encore question des gens.' [This translates as 'I hate like death the idea that people
of his own age might believe me to have liaisons. To all appearances
one is deemed to be a hundred years old the moment one is older than
they – and they are all too prone to wonder at there still being men
['gens' may be translated in various ways] about one.' (Editors).]

survive show that she excelled in that epistolary style which was the speciality of the Hôtel de Rambouillet; one to Madame de Montausier, in favour of M. Périer, the brother-in-law of Pascal, is a happy mixture of good taste and good sense; but amongst them all we prefer quoting one to the Duchesse de la Trimouille. It is light and pretty, and made out of almost nothing, like soap-bubbles.

Je crois qu'il n'y a que moi qui face si bien tout le con-traire de ce que je veux faire, car il est vrai qu'il n'y a per-sonne que j'honore plus que vous et j'ai si bien fait qu'il est quasi impossible que vous le puissiez croire. Ce n'estoit pas assez pour vous persuader que je suis indigne de vos bonnes grâces et de votre souvenir que d'avoir manqué fort longtemps à vous écrire; il falloit encore retarder quinze jours à me donner l'honneur de répondre à votre lettre. En vérité, madame, cela me fait parôître si coup-able, que vers tout autre que vous j'aimerois mieux l'etre en effet que d'entreprendre une chose si difficile qu'est celle de me justifier. Mais je me sens si innocente dans mon âme, et j'ai tant d'estime, de respect et d'affection pour vous, qu'il me semble que vous devez le connôitre à cent lieues de distance d'ici, encore que je ne vous dise pas un mot. C'est ce que me donne le courage de vous écrire à cette heure, mais non pas ce qui m'en a empêché si longtemps. J'ai commencé à faillir par force, ayant eu beaucoup de maux, et depuis je l'ai fait par honte, et je vous avoue que si je n'avois à cette heure la confiance que vous m'avez donnée en me rassurant, et celle que je tire de mes propres sentiments pour vous, je n'oserois jamais entreprendre de vous faire souvenir de moi; mais

je m'assure que vous oublierez tout, sur la protestation
que je vous fais de ne me laisser plus endurceir en mes
fautes et de demeurer inviolablement, madame, votre, etc.

Was not the woman, who could unite the ease and
grace indicated by this letter, with an intellect that men
thought worth consulting on matters of reasoning and
philosophy, with warm affections, untiring activity for
others, no ambition as an authoress, and an insight into
confitures and *ragoûts*, a rare combination? No wonder
that her *salon* at Port-Royal was the favourite resort of
such women as Madame de la Fayette, Madame de Montausier, Madame de Longueville, and Madame de Haute-
fort; and of such men as Pascal, La Rochefoucauld, Nicole,
and Domat. The collections of Valant contain papers which
show what were the habitual subjects of conversation in
this *salon*. Theology, of course, was a chief topic; but phys-
ics and metaphysics had their turn, and still more frequently
morals, taken in their widest sense. There were *Conferences on Calvinism*, of which an abstract is preserved. When
Rohault invented his glass tubes to serve for the baromet-
rical experiments, in which Pascal had roused a strong interest, the Marquis de Sourdis entertained the society with a
paper, entitled *Why Water Mounts in a Glass Tube*. Cartes-
ianism was an exciting topic here, as well as everywhere
else in France; it had its partisans and opponents; and
papers were read, containing *Thoughts on the Opinions of
M. Descartes*. These lofty matters were varied by discus-
sions on love and friendship, on the drama, and on most
of the things in heaven and earth which the philosophy
of that day dreamt of. Morals – generalizations on human

affections, sentiments, and conduct – seem to have been the favourite theme; and the aim was to reduce these generalizations to their briefest form of expression, to give them the epigrammatic turn which made them portable in the memory. This was the specialty of Madame de Sablé's circle, and was, probably, due to her own tendency. As the Hôtel de Rambouillet was the nursery of graceful letter-writing, and the Luxembourg of 'portraits' and 'characters', so Madame de Sablé's *salon* fostered that taste for the sententious style, to which we owe, probably, some of the best *Pensées* of Pascal, and, certainly, the *Maximes* of La Rochefoucauld. Madame de Sablé herself wrote maxims, which were circulated among her friends; and, after her death, were published by the Abbé d'Ailly. They have the excellent sense and nobility of feeling which we should expect in everything of hers; but they have no stamp of genius or individual character: they are, to the *Maximes* of La Rochefoucauld, what the vase moulded in dull, heavy clay, is to the vase which the action of fire has made light, brittle, and transparent. She also wrote a treatise on Education, which is much praised by La Rochefoucauld and M. d'Andilly; but which seems no longer to be found: probably it was not much more elaborate than her so-called 'Treatise on Friendship', which is but a short string of maxims. Madame de Sablé's forte was evidently not to write herself, but to stimulate others to write; to show that sympathy and appreciation which are as genial and encouraging as the morning sunbeams. She seconded a man's wit with understanding – one of the best offices which womanly intellect has rendered to the advancement of culture; and the absence of originality made her all the more receptive towards the originality of others.

The manuscripts of Pascal show that many of the *Pensées*, which are commonly supposed to be raw materials for a great work on religion, were remodelled again and again, in order to bring them to the highest degree of terseness and finish, which would hardly have been the case if they had only been part of a quarry for a greater production. Thoughts which are merely collected as materials, as stones out of which a building is to be erected, are not cut into facets, and polished like amethysts or emeralds. Since Pascal was from the first in the habit of visiting Madame de Sablé at Port-Royal, with his sister, Madame Périer (who was one of Madame de Sablé's dearest friends), we may well suppose that he would throw some of his jewels among the large and small coin of maxims, which were a sort of subscription-money there. Many of them have an epigrammatic piquancy, which was just the thing to charm a circle of vivacious and intelligent women; they seem to come from a La Rochefoucauld, who has been dipped over again in philosophy and wit, and received a new layer. But whether or not Madame de Sablé's influence served to enrich the *Pensées* of Pascal, it is clear that but for her influence the *Maximes* of La Rochefoucauld would never have existed. Just as in some circles the effort is, who shall make the best puns (*horribile dictu!*), or the best charades, in the *salon* of Port-Royal the amusement was to fabricate maxims. La Rochefoucauld said, 'L'envie de faire des maximes se gagne comme le rhume.' So far from claiming for himself the initiation of this form of writing, he accuses Jacques Esprit, another *habitué* of Madame de Sablé's *salon*, of having excited in him the taste for maxims, in order to trouble his repose. The said Esprit was an academician, and had been a frequenter of the Hôtel de Rambouillet. He had already published *Maximes en vers*, and he subsequently produced a book called *La Fausseté des vertus humaines*, which seems to consist of Rochefoucauldism become flat with an infusion of sour Calvinism. Nevertheless, La Rochefoucauld seems to have prized him, to have appealed to his judgement, and to have concocted maxims with him, which he afterwards begs him to submit to Madame de Sablé. He sends a little batch of maxims to her himself, and asks for an equivalent in the shape of good eatables: 'Voilà tout ce que j'ai de maximes; mais comme je ne donne rien pour rien, je vous demande un potage aux carottes, un ragoût de mouton,' etc. The taste and the talent enhanced each other; until, at last, La Rochefoucauld began to be conscious of his pre-eminence in the circle of maxim-mongers, and thought of a wider audience. Thus grew up the famous *Maximes*, about which little need be said. Every one is now convinced, or professes to be convinced, that, as to form, they are perfect, and that as to matter, they are at once undeniably true and miserably false; true as applied to that condition of human nature in which the selfish instincts are still dominant, false if taken as a representation of all the elements and possibilities of human nature. We think La Rochefoucauld himself wavered as to their universality, and that this wavering is indicated in the qualified form of some of the maxims; it occasionally struck him that the shadow of virtue must have a substance, but he had never grasped that substance – it had never been present to his consciousness.

It is curious to see La Rochefoucauld's nervous anxiety about presenting himself before the public as an author; far from rushing into print, he stole into it, and felt his way by asking private opinions. Through Madame de Sablé he sent manuscript copies to various persons of taste and talent, both men and women, and many of the written opinions which she received in reply are still in existence. The women generally find the maxims distasteful, but the men write approvingly. These men, however, are for the most part ecclesiastics who decry human nature that they may exalt divine grace. The coincidence between Augustinianism or Calvinism, with its doctrine of human corruption, and the hard cynicism of the maxims, presents itself in quite a piquant form in some of the laudatory opinions of La Rochefoucauld. One writer says: – 'On ne pourroit faire une instruction plus propre à un catéchumène pour convertir à Dieu son esprit et sa volonté . . . Quand il n'y auroit que cet escrit au monde et l'Evangile je voudrois être chrétien. L'un m'apprendroit à connoistre mes misères, et l'autre à implorer mon libérateur.' Madame de Maintenon sends word to La Rochefoucauld, after the publication of his work, that the Book of Job and the *Maximes* are her only reading!

That Madame de Sablé herself had a tolerably just idea of La Rochefoucauld's character, as well as of his maxims, may be gathered not only from the fact that her own maxims are as full of the confidence in human goodness which La Rochefoucauld wants, as they are empty of the style which he possesses, but also from a letter in which she replies to the criticisms of Madame de Schomberg. 'The author,' she says, 'derived the maxim on indolence from his own disposition, for never was there so great an indolence as his, and I think that his heart, inert as it is, owes this defect as much to his idleness as his will. It has never permitted him to do the last action for others; and I think that, amidst all his great desires and great hopes, he is sometimes indolent even on his own behalf.' Still she must have felt a hearty interest in the *Maximes*, as in some degree her foster-child, and she must also have had considerable affection for the author, who was lovable enough to those who observed the rule of Helvetius, and expected nothing from him. She not only assisted him, as we have seen, in getting criticisms, and carrying out the improvements suggested by them, but when the book was actually published, she prepared a notice of it for the only journal then existing – the *Journal des savants*. This notice was originally a brief statement of the nature of the work, and the opinions which had been formed for and against it, with a moderate eulogy, in conclusion, on its good sense, wit, and insight into human nature. But when she submitted it to La Rochefoucauld he objected to the paragraph which stated the adverse opinion, and requested her to alter it. She, however, was either unable or unwilling to modify her notice, and returned it with the following note:–

Je vous envoie ce que j'ai pu tirer de ma teste pour mettre dans le *Journal des savants*. J'y ai mis cet endroit qui vous est le plus sensible, afin que cela vous fasse surmonter la mauvaise honte qui vous fit mettre la préface sans y rien retrancher, et je n'ai pas craint de le mettre, parce que je suis assurée que vous ne le ferez pas imprimer, quand même le reste vous plairoit. Je vous assure aussi que je vous serai plus obligée, si vous en usez comme d'une chose qui servit à vous pour le corriger ou pour le jeter au feu. Nous autres grands auteurs, nous sommes trop riches pour craindre de rien perdre de nos productions. Mandez-moi ce qu'il vous semble de ce dictum.

La Rochefoucauld availed himself of this permission, and 'edited' the notice, touching up the style, and leaving out the blame. In this revised form it appeared in the *Journal des savants*. In some points, we see, the youth of journalism was not without promise of its future.

While Madame de Sablé was thus playing the literary confidante to La Rochefoucauld, and was the soul of a society whose chief interest was the *belles lettres*, she was equally active in graver matters. She was in constant intercourse or correspondence with the devout women of Port-Royal, and of the neighbouring convent of the Carmelites, many of whom had once been the ornaments of the court; and there is a proof that she was conscious of being highly valued by them in the fact that when the Princess Marie-Madeline, of the Carmelites, was dangerously ill, not being able or not daring to visit her, she sent her youthful portrait to be hung up in the sick-room, and received from the same Mère Agnés whose grave admonition we have quoted above, a charming note, describing the pleasure which the picture had given in the infirmary of 'Notre bonne Mère'. She was interesting herself deeply in the translation of the New Testament, which was the work of Sacy, Arnauld, Nicole, Le Maître, and the Duc de Luynes conjointly, Sacy having the principal share. We have mentioned that Arnauld asked her opinion on the Discourse prefixed to his *Logic*, and we may conclude from this that he had found her judgement valuable in many other cases. Moreover, the persecution of the Port-Royalists had commenced, and she was uniting with Madame de Longueville in aiding and protecting her pious friends. Moderate in her Jansenism, as in everything else, she held that the famous formulary denouncing the Augustinian doctrine, and declaring it to have been originated by Jansenius, should be signed without reserve, and, as usual, she had faith in conciliatory measures; but her moderation was no excuse for inaction. She was at one time herself threatened with the necessity of abandoning her residence at Port-Royal, and had thought of retiring to a religious house at Auteuil, a village near Paris. She did, in fact, pass some summers there, and she sometimes took refuge with her brother, the Commandeur de Souvré, with Madame de Montausier, or Madame de Longueville. The last was much bolder in her partisanship than her friend, and her superior wealth and position enabled her to give the Port-Royalists more efficient aid. Arnauld and Nicole resided five years in her house; it was under her protection that the translation of the New Testament was carried on and completed, and it was chiefly through her efforts that, in 1669, the persecution was brought to an end. Madame de Sablé co-operated with all her talent and interest in the same direction; but here, as elsewhere, her influence was chiefly valuable in what she stimulated others to do, rather than in what she did herself. It was by her that Madame de Longueville was first won to the cause of Port-Royal; and we find this ardent brave woman constantly seeking the advice and sympathy of her more timid and self-indulgent, but sincere and judicious friend.

In 1669, when Madame de Sablé had at length rest from these anxieties, she was at the good old age of seventy, but she lived nine years longer – years, we may suppose, chiefly dedicated to her spiritual concerns. This gradual, calm decay allayed the fear of death which had tormented her more vigorous days; and she died with tranquillity and trust. It is a beautiful trait of these last moments, that she desired not to be buried with her family, or even at Port-Royal, among her saintly and noble companions, but in the cemetery of her parish, like one of the people, without pomp or ceremony.

It is worth while to notice, that with Madame de Sablé, as with some other remarkable French women, the part of her life which is richest in interest and results, is that which is looked forward to by most of her sex with melancholy as the period of decline. When between fifty and sixty, she had philosophers, wits, beauties, and saints clustering around her; and one naturally cares to know what was the elixir which gave her this enduring and general attraction. We think it was, in a great degree, that well-balanced development of mental powers which gave her a comprehension of varied intellectual processes, and a tolerance for varied forms of character, which is still rarer in women than in men. Here was one point of distinction between her and Madame de Longueville; and an amusing passage, which Sainte-Beuve has disinterred from the writings of the Abbé St Pierre, so well serves to indicate, by contrast, what we regard as the great charm of Madame de Sablé's mind, that we shall not be wandering from our subject in quoting it.

I one day asked M. Nicole what was the character of Madame de Longueville's intellect; he told me it was very subtle and delicate in the penetration of character, but very small, very feeble; and that her comprehension was extremely narrow in matters of science and reasoning, and on all speculations that did not concern matters of sentiment. For example, he added, I one day said to her that I could wager and demonstrate that there were in Paris, at least two inhabitants who had the same number of hairs, although I could not point out who these two men were. She told me, I could never be sure of it until I had counted the hairs of these two men. Here is my demonstration, I said: – I take it for granted that the head which is most amply supplied with hairs has not more than 200,000 and the head which is least so has but one hair. Now, if you suppose that 200,000 heads have each a different number of hairs, it necessarily follows that they have each one of the numbers of hairs which form the series from 1 to 200,000; for if it were supposed that there were two among these 200,000 who had the same number of hairs, I should have gained my wager. Supposing, then, that these 200,000 inhabitants have all a different number of hairs, if I add a single inhabitant who has hairs, and who has not more than 200,000, it necessarily follows that this number of hairs, whatever

it may be, will be contained in the series from 1 to
200,000, and consequently will be equal to the number
of hairs on one of the previous 200,000 inhabitants. Now
as, instead of one inhabitant more than 200,000, there
are nearly 800,000 inhabitants in Paris, you see clearly
that there must be many heads which have an equal
number of hairs, though I have not counted them. Still
Madame de Longueville could never comprehend that
this equality of hairs could be demonstrated, and always
maintained that the only way of proving it was to count
them.

Surely, the most ardent admirer of feminine shallowness
must have felt some irritation when he found himself
arrested by this dead wall of stupidity, and have turned
with relief to the larger intelligence of Madame de Sablé,
who was not the less graceful, delicate, and feminine,
because she could follow a train of reasoning, or interest
herself in a question of science. In this combination con-
sisted her pre-eminent charm: she was not a genius, not
a heroine, but a woman whom men could more than
love – whom they could make their friend, confidante,
and counsellor; the sharer, not of their joys and sorrows
only, but of their ideas and aims.

Such was Madame de Sablé, whose name is, perhaps,
new to some of our readers, so far does it lie from the sur-
face of literature and history. We have seen, too, that she
was only one amongst a crowd – one in a firmament of
feminine stars which, when once the biographical tele-
scope is turned upon them, appear scarcely less remarkable
and interesting. Now, if the reader recollects what was the

position and average intellectual character of women in the high society of England during the reigns of James I and the two Charleses – the period through which Madame de Sablé's career extends – we think he will admit our position as to the early superiority of womanly development in France: and this fact, with its causes, has not merely an historical interest, it has an important bearing on the culture of women in the present day. Women become superior in France by being admitted to a common fund of ideas, to common objects of interest with men; and this must ever be the essential condition at once of true womanly culture and of true social well-being. We have no faith in feminine conversazioni, where ladies are eloquent on Apollo and Mars; though we sympathize with the yearning activity of faculties which, deprived of their proper material, waste themselves in weaving fabrics out of cobwebs. Let the whole field of reality be laid open to woman as well as to man, and then that which is peculiar in her mental modification, instead of being, as it is now, a source of discord and repulsion between the sexes, will be found to be a necessary complement to the truth and beauty of life. Then we shall have that marriage of minds which alone can blend all the hues of thought and feeling in one lovely rainbow of promise for the harvest of human happiness.

Geraldine Jewsbury's
Constance Herbert

Next in interest to *Westward Ho!* at least among the English novels of the quarter, is *Constance Herbert*. Miss Jewsbury has created precedents for herself which make critics exacting towards her. We measure her work by her own standard, and find it deficient; when if measured by the standard of ordinary feminine novelists, it would perhaps seem excellent. We meet with some beauties in it which, coming from the author of the *Half Sisters*, we take as a matter of course, but we miss other beauties which she has taught us to expect; we feel that she is not equal to herself; and it is a tribute to her well-attested powers if we dwell on what has disappointed us, rather than on what has gratified us. An easy, agreeable style of narrative, some noble sentiments expressed in the quiet, unexaggerated way that indicates their source to be a deep spring of conviction and experience, not a mere rain-torrent of hearsay enthusiasm, with here and there a trait of character or conduct painted with the truthfulness of close observation, are merits enough to raise a book far above the common run of circulating library fiction; but they are not enough to make a good novel, or one worthy of Miss Jewsbury's reputation. *Constance Herbert* is a *Tendenz-roman*; the characters and incidents are selected with a view to the enforcement of a principle. The general principle meant to be enforced is the unhesitating, uncompromising sacrifice of inclination to duty, and the special case to which this principle is applied in the novel, is the abstinence from marriage where there is an inheritance of insanity. So far, we have no difference of opinion with Miss Jewsbury. But the *mode* in which she enforces the principle, both theoretically in the *Envoi* and illustratively in the story of her novel, implies, we think, a false view of life, and virtually nullifies the very magnanimity she inculcates. 'If,' she says in the *Envoi*, 'we have succeeded in articulating any principle in this book, it is to entreat our readers to have boldness to act up to the sternest requirements that duty claims as right. Although it may at the time seem to slay them, it will in the end prove life. *Nothing they renounce for the sake of a higher principle, will prove to have been worth the keeping.*' The italics are ours, and we use them to indicate what we think false in Miss Jewsbury's moral. This moral is illustrated in the novel by the story of three ladies, who, after renouncing their lovers, or being renounced by them, have the satisfaction of feeling in the end that these lovers were extremely 'good-for-nothing', and that they (the ladies) have had an excellent riddance. In all this we can see neither the true doctrine of renunciation, nor a true representation of the realities of life; and we are sorry that a writer of Miss Jewsbury's insight and sincerity should have produced three volumes for the sake of teaching such copy-book morality. It is not the fact that what duty calls on us to renounce, will invariably prove 'not worth the keeping'; and if it *were* the fact, renunciation would cease to be moral heroism, and would be simply a calculation of prudence. Let us take the special case which

Miss Jewsbury has chosen as her illustration. It might equally happen that a woman in the position of Constance Herbert, who renounces marriage because she will not entail on others the family heritage of insanity, had fixed her affections, not on an egotistic, shallow worldling like Philip Marchmont, but on a man who was fitted to make the happiness of a woman's life, and whose subsequent career would only impress on her more and more deeply the extent of the sacrifice she had made in refusing him. And it is this very perception that the thing we renounce is precious, is something never to be compensated to us, which constitutes the beauty and heroism of renunciation. The only motive that renders such a resolution as Constance Herbert's noble, is that keen sympathy with human misery which makes a woman prefer to suffer for the term of her own life, rather than run the risk of causing misery to an indefinite number of other human beings; and a mind influenced by such a motive will find no support in the very questionable satisfaction of discovering that objects once cherished were in fact worthless. The notion that duty looks stern, but all the while has her hand full of sugar-plums, with which she will reward us by and by, is the favourite cant of optimists, who try to make out that this tangled wilderness of life has a plan as easy to trace as that of a Dutch garden; but it really undermines all true moral development by perpetually substituting something extrinsic as a motive to action, instead of the immediate impulse of love or justice, which alone makes an action truly moral. This is a grave question to enter on *à propos* of a novel; but Miss Jewsbury is so emphatic in the enunciation of her moral, that she forces us to consider her book rather in the light of a homily than of a fiction – to criticize her doctrine rather than her story. On another point, too, we must remonstrate with her a little, chiefly because we value her influence, and should like to see it always in what seems to us the right scale. With the exception of Mr Harrop, who is simply a cipher awaiting a wife to give him any value, there is not a man in her book who is not either weak, perfidious, or rascally, while almost all the women are models of magnanimity and devotedness. The lions, i.e., the ladies, have got the brush in their hands with a vengeance now, and are retaliating for the calumnies of men from Adam downwards. Perhaps it is but fair to allow them a little exaggeration. Still we must meekly suggest that we cannot accept an *ex parte* statement, even from that paragon Aunt Margaret, as altogether decisive. Aunt Margaret tells us that in the bloom of youth and beauty, with virtues and accomplishments to correspond, she alienated her husband by pure devotion to him. 'No man,' she says, 'can bear entire devotion.' This reminds us of a certain toper, who after drinking a series of glasses of brandy-and-water one night, complained the next morning that the water did not agree with him. We are inclined to think that it is less frequently devotion which alienates men, than something infused in the devotion – a certain amount of silliness, or temper, or *exigeance*, for example, which, though given in small doses, will, if persevered in, have a strongly alterative effect. Men, in fact, are in rather a difficult position: in one ear a Miss Grace Lee, or some such strong-minded woman, thunders that they demand to be worshipped, and abhor a woman who has any self-dependence; on the other, a melancholy Viola complains that they never appreciate devotion, that they care only for a woman who treats them with indifference. A discouraging view of the case for both sexes! Seriously, we care too much for the attainment of a better understanding as to woman's true position, not to be sorry when a writer like Miss Jewsbury only adds her voice to swell the confusion on this subject.

Margaret Fuller and Mary Wollstonecraft

The dearth of new books just now gives us time to recur to less recent ones which we have hitherto noticed but slightly; and among these we choose the late edition of Margaret Fuller's *Woman in the Nineteenth Century*, because we think it has been unduly thrust into the background by less comprehensive and candid productions on the same subject. Notwithstanding certain defects of taste and a sort of vague spiritualism and grandiloquence which belong to all but the very best American writers, the book is a valuable one: it has the enthusiasm of a noble and sympathetic nature, with the moderation and breadth and large allowance of a vigorous and cultivated understanding. There is no exaggeration of woman's moral excellence or intellectual capabilities; no injudicious insistence on her fitness for this or that function hitherto engrossed by men; but a calm plea for the removal of unjust laws and artificial restrictions, so that the possibilities of her nature may have room for full development, a wisely stated demand to disencumber her of the

> Parasitic forms
> That seem to keep her up, but drag her down –
> And leave her field to burgeon and to bloom
> From all within her, make herself her own

To give or keep, to live and learn and be
All that not harms distinctive womanhood.

It is interesting to compare this essay of Margaret
Fuller's, published in its earliest form in 1843, with a work
on the position of woman, written between sixty and
seventy years ago – we mean Mary Wollstonecraft's
Rights of Woman. The latter work was not continued
beyond the first volume; but so far as this carries the subject, the comparison, at least in relation to strong sense
and loftiness of moral tone, is not at all disadvantageous
to the woman of the last century. There is in some quar-
ters a vague prejudice against the *Rights of Woman* as in
some way or other a reprehensible book, but readers
who go to it with this impression will be surprised to find
it eminently serious, severely moral, and withal rather
heavy – the true reason, perhaps, that no edition has
been published since 1796, and that it is now rather scarce.
There are several points of resemblance, as well as of
striking difference, between the two books. A strong
understanding is present in both; but Margaret Fuller's
mind was like some regions of her own American contin-
ent, where you are constantly stepping from the sunny
'clearings' into the mysterious twilight of the tangled
forest – she often passes in one breath from forcible reasoning to dreamy vagueness; moreover, her unusually
varied culture gives her great command of illustration.
Mary Wollstonecraft, on the other hand, is nothing if not
rational; she has no erudition, and her grave pages are lit
up by no ray of fancy. In both writers we discern, under
the brave bearing of a strong and truthful nature, the

beating of a loving woman's heart, which teaches them not to undervalue the smallest offices of domestic care or kindliness. But Margaret Fuller, with all her passionate sensibility, is more of the literary woman, who would not have been satisfied without intellectual production; Mary Wollstonecraft, we imagine, wrote not at all for writing's sake, but from the pressure of other motives. So far as the difference of date allows, there is a striking coincidence in their trains of thought; indeed, every important idea in the *Rights of Woman*, except the combination of home education with a common day-school for boys and girls, reappears in Margaret Fuller's essay.

One point on which they both write forcibly is the fact that, while men have a horror of such faculty or culture in the other sex as tends to place it on a level with their own, they are really in a state of subjection to ignorant and feeble-minded women. Margaret Fuller says: –

Wherever man is sufficiently raised above extreme poverty or brutal stupidity, to care for the comforts of the fireside, or the bloom and ornament of life, woman has always power enough, if she choose to exert it, and is usually disposed to do so, in proportion to her ignorance and childish vanity. Unacquainted with the importance of life and its purposes, trained to a selfish coquetry and love of petty power, she does not look beyond the pleasure of making herself felt at the moment, and governments are shaken and commerce broken up to gratify the pique of a female favourite. The English shopkeeper's wife does not vote, but it is for her interest that the politician canvasses by the coarsest flattery.

Again: –

> All wives, bad or good, loved or unloved, inevitably influ-
> ence their husbands from the power their position not
> merely gives, but necessitates of colouring evidence and
> infusing feelings in hours when the – patient, shall I call
> him? – is off his guard.

Hear now what Mary Wollstonecraft says on the same
subject: –

> Women have been allowed to remain in ignorance and
> slavish dependence many, very many years, and still
> we hear of nothing but their fondness of pleasure and
> sway, their preference of rakes and soldiers, their childish
> attachment to toys, and the vanity that makes them
> value accomplishments more than virtues. History brings
> forward a fearful catalogue of the crimes which their
> cunning has produced, when the weak slaves have had
> sufficient address to overreach their masters . . . When,
> therefore, I call women slaves, I mean in a political and
> civil sense; for indirectly they obtain too much power,
> and are debased by their exertions to obtain illicit sway . . .
> The libertinism, and even the virtues of superior men,
> will always give women of some description great power
> over them; and these weak women, under the influence
> of childish passions and selfish vanity, *will throw a false
> light over the objects which the very men view with their eyes
> who ought to enlighten their judgement.* Men of fancy, and
> those sanguine characters who mostly hold the helm of
> human affairs in general, relax in the society of women;

and surely I need not cite to the most superficial reader of history the numerous examples of vice and oppression which the private intrigues of female favourites have produced; not to dwell on the mischief that naturally arises from the blundering interposition of well-meaning folly. *For in the transactions of business it is much better to have to deal with a knave than a fool, because a knave adheres to some plan, and any plan of reason may be seen through sooner than a sudden flight of folly.* The power which vile and foolish women have had over wise men who possessed sensibility is notorious.

There is a notion commonly entertained among men that an instructed woman, capable of having opinions, is likely to prove an impracticable yoke-fellow, always pulling one way when her husband wants to go the other, oracular in tone, and prone to give curtain lectures on metaphysics. But surely, so far as obstinacy is concerned, your unreasoning animal is the most unmanageable of creatures, where you are not allowed to settle the question by a cudgel, a whip and bridle, or even a string to the leg. For our own parts, we see no consistent or commodious medium between the old plan of corporal discipline and that thorough education of women which will make them rational beings in the highest sense of the word. Wherever weakness is not harshly controlled it must *govern*, as you may see when a strong man holds a little child by the hand, how he is pulled hither and thither, and wearied in his walk by his submission to the whims and feeble movements of his companion. A really cultured woman, like a really cultured man, will be ready to yield in trifles.

So far as we see, there is no indissoluble connexion between infirmity of logic and infirmity of will, and a woman quite innocent of an opinion in philosophy, is as likely as not to have an indomitable opinion about the kitchen. As to airs of superiority, no woman ever had them in consequence of true culture, but only because her culture was shallow or unreal, only as a result of what Mrs Malaprop well calls 'the ineffectual qualities in a woman' – mere acquisitions carried about, and not knowledge thoroughly assimilated so as to enter into the growth of the character.

To return to Margaret Fuller, some of the best things she says are on the folly of absolute definitions of woman's nature and absolute demarcations of woman's mission. 'Nature,' she says, 'seems to delight in varying the arrangements, as if to show that she will be fettered by no rule; and we must admit the same varieties that she admits.' Again: 'If nature is never bound down, nor the voice of inspiration stifled, that is enough. We are pleased that women should write and speak, if they feel need of it, from having something to tell; but silence for ages would be no misfortune, if that silence be from divine command, and not from man's tradition.' And here is a passage, the beginning of which has been often quoted: –

If you ask me what offices they (women) may fill, I reply – any. I do not care what case you put; let them be sea-captains if you will. I do not doubt there are women well fitted for such an office, and, if so, I should be as glad as to welcome the Maid of Saragossa, or the Maid of Missolonghi, or the Suliote heroine, or Emily Plater. I think women need, especially at this juncture, a much greater range of occupation than they have, to rouse their latent powers . . . In families that I know, some little girls like to saw wood, others to use carpenter's tools. Where these tastes are indulged, cheerfulness and good-humour are promoted. Where they are forbidden, because 'such things are not proper for girls', they grow sullen and mischievous. Fourier had observed these wants of women, as no one can fail to do who watches the desires of little girls, or knows the *ennui* that haunts grown women, except where they make to themselves a serene little world by art of some kind. He, therefore, in proposing a great variety of employments, in manufactures or the care of plants and animals, allows for one third of women as likely to have a taste for masculine pursuits, one third of men for feminine . . . I have no doubt, however, that a large proportion of women would give themselves to the same employments as now, because there are circumstances that must lead them. Mothers will delight to make the nest soft and warm. Nature would take care of that; no need to clip the wings of any bird that wants to soar and sing, or finds in itself the strength of pinion for a migratory flight unusual to its kind. The difference would be that *all* need not be constrained to employments for which *some* are unfit.

A propos of the same subject, we find Mary Wollstonecraft offering a suggestion which the women of the United States have already begun to carry out. She says: –

Women, in particular, all want to be ladies. Which is simply to have nothing to do, but listlessly to go they scarcely care where, for they cannot tell what. But what have women to do in society? I may be asked, but to loiter with easy grace; surely you would not condemn them all to suckle fools and chronicle small beer. No. *Women might certainly study the art of healing, and be physicians as well as nurses* . . . Business of various kinds they might likewise pursue, if they were educated in a more orderly manner . . . Women would not then marry for a support, as men accept of places under government, and neglect the implied duties.

Men pay a heavy price for their reluctance to encourage self-help and independent resources in women. The precious meridian years of many a man of genius have to be spent in the toil of routine, that an 'establishment' may be kept up for a woman who can understand none of his secret yearnings, who is fit for nothing but to sit in her drawing-room like a doll-Madonna in her shrine. No matter. Anything is more endurable than to change our established formulæ about women, or to run the risk of looking up to our wives instead of looking down on them. *Sit divus, dummodo non sit vivus* (let him be a god, provided he be not living), said the Roman magnates of Romulus; and so men say of women, let them be idols, useless absorbents of precious things, provided we are not obliged to admit them to be strictly fellow-beings, to be treated, one and all, with justice and sober reverence.

On one side we hear that woman's position can never be improved until women themselves are better; and, on the other, that women can never become better until their position is improved – until the laws are made more just, and a wider field opened to feminine activity. But we constantly hear the same difficulty stated about the human race in general. There is a perpetual action and reaction between individuals and institutions; we must try and mend both by little and little – the only way in which human things can be mended. Unfortunately, many over-zealous champions of women assert their actual equality with men – nay, even their moral superiority to men – as a ground for their release from oppressive laws and restrictions. They lose strength immensely by this false position. If it were true, then there would be a case in which slavery and ignorance nourished virtue, and so far we should have an argument for the continuance of bondage. But we want freedom and culture for woman, because subjection and ignorance have debased her, and with her, Man; for –

> If she be small, slight-natured, miserable,
> How shall men grow?

Both Margaret Fuller and Mary Wollstonecraft have too much sagacity to fall into this sentimental exaggeration. Their ardent hopes of what women may become do not prevent them from seeing and painting women as they are. On the relative moral excellence of men and women Mary Wollstonecraft speaks with the most decision: –

Women are supposed to possess more sensibility, and even humanity, than men, and their strong attachments and instantaneous emotions of compassion are given as proofs; but the clinging affection of ignorance has seldom anything noble in it, and may mostly be resolved into selfishness, as well as the affection of children and brutes. I have known many weak women whose sensibility was entirely engrossed by their husbands; and as for their humanity, it was very faint indeed, or rather it was only a transient emotion of compassion. Humanity does not consist 'in a squeamish ear', says an eminent orator. 'It belongs to the mind as well as to the nerves.' But this kind of exclusive affection, though it degrades the individual, should not be brought forward as a proof of the inferiority of the sex, because it is the natural consequence of confined views; for even women of superior sense, having their attention turned to little employments and private plans, rarely rise to heroism, unless when spurred on by love! and love, as an heroic passion, like genius, appears but once in an age. I therefore agree with the moralist who asserts 'that women have seldom so much generosity as men'; and that their narrow affections, to which justice and humanity are often sacrificed, render the sex apparently inferior, especially as they are commonly inspired by men; but I contend that the heart would expand as the understanding gained strength, if women were not depressed from their cradles.

We had marked several other passages of Margaret Fuller's for extract, but as we do not aim at an exhaustive treatment of our subject, and are only touching a few of its points, we have, perhaps, already claimed as much of the reader's attention as he will be willing to give to such desultory material.

Harriet Beecher Stowe's Dred, Charles Reade's It is Never Too Late to Mend *and Frederika Bremer's* Hertha

At length we have Mrs Stowe's new novel, and for the last three weeks there have been men, women, and children reading it with rapt attention – laughing and sobbing over it – lingering with delight over its exquisite land-scapes, its scenes of humour, and tenderness, and rude heroism – and glowing with indignation at its terrible representation of chartered barbarities. Such a book is an uncontrollable power, and critics who follow it with their objections and reservations – who complain that Mrs Stowe's plot is defective, that she has repeated her-self, that her book is too long and too full of hymns and religious dialogue, and that it creates an unfair bias – are something like men pursuing a prairie fire with desultory watering-cans. In the meantime, *Dred* will be devoured by the million, who carry no critical talisman against the enchantments of genius. We confess ourselves to be among the million, and quite unfit to rank with the sage minority of Fadladeens. We have been too much moved by *Dred* to determine with precision how far it is inferior to *Uncle Tom*, too much impressed by what Mrs Stowe *has* done to be quite sure that we can tell her what she ought to have done. Our admiration of the book is quite distinct from any opinions or hesitations we may have as to the terribly difficult problems of Slavery and Abolition – problems which belong to quite other than 'polite literature'. Even admitting Mrs Stowe to be mistaken in her views, and partial or exaggerated in her representations, *Dred* remains not the less a novel inspired by a rare genius – rare both in intensity and in range of power.

Looking at the matter simply from an artistic point of view, we see no reason to regret that Mrs Stowe should keep to her original ground of Negro and planter life, any more than that Scott should have introduced Highland life into *Rob Roy* and *The Fair Maid of Perth*, when he had already written *Waverley*. Mrs Stowe has *invented* the Negro novel, and it is a novel not only fresh in its scenery and its manners, but possessing that *conflict of races* which Augustin Thierry has pointed out as the great source of romantic interest – witness *Ivanhoe*. Inventions in literature are not as plentiful as inventions in the paletot and waterproof department, and it is rather amusing that we reviewers, who have, for the most part, to read nothing but imitations of imitations, should put on airs of tolerance towards Mrs Stowe because she has written a second Negro novel, and make excuses for her on the ground that she perhaps would not succeed in any other kind of fiction. Probably she would not; for her genius seems to be of a very special character: her *Sunny Memories* were as feeble as her novels are powerful. But whatever else she may write, or may not write, *Uncle Tom* and *Dred* will assure her a place in that highest rank of novelists who can give us a national life in all its phases – popular and aristocratic, humorous and tragic, political and religious.

But Mrs Stowe's novels have not only that grand element – conflict of races; they have another element equally grand, which she also shares with Scott, and in which she has, in some respects, surpassed him. This is the exhibition of a people to whom what we may call Hebraic Christianity is still a reality, still an animating belief, and by whom the theocratic conceptions of the Old Testament are literally applied to their daily life. Where has Scott done anything finer than the character of Balfour of Burley, the battles of Drumclog and Bothwell Brigg, and the trial of Ephraim MacBriar? And the character of Dred, the death scenes in the Swamp, and the Camp Meeting of Presbyterians and Methodists, will bear comparison – if we except the fighting – with the best parts of *Old Mortality*. The strength of Mrs Stowe's own religious feeling is a great artistic advantage to her here; she never makes you feel that she is coldly calculating an effect, but you see that she is all a-glow for the moment with the wild enthusiasm, the unreasoning faith, and the steady martyr-spirit of Dred, of Tiff, or of Father Dickson. But with this, she has the keen sense of humour which preserves her from extravagance and monotony; and though she paints her religious Negroes *en beau*, they are always specifically Negroes – she never loses hold of her characters, and lets dramatic dialogue merge into vague oratory. Indeed, here is her strongest point: her dramatic instinct is always awake; and whether it is the grotesque Old Tiff or the aërial Nina, the bluff sophist Father Bonim or the gentlemanly sophist Frank Russell, her characters are always like themselves; a quality which is all the more remarkable in novels animated by a vehement polemical purpose.

The objection which is patent to every one who looks at Mrs Stowe's novels in an argumentative light, is also, we think, one of their artistic defects; namely, the absence of any proportionate exhibition of the Negro character in its less amiable phases. Judging from her pictures, one would conclude that the Negro race was vastly superior to the mass of whites, even in other than slave countries – a state of the case which would singularly defeat Mrs Stowe's sarcasms on the cant of those who call slavery a 'Christianizing Institution'. If the Negroes are really so very good, slavery has answered as moral discipline. But apart from the argumentative suicide involved in this one-sidedness, Mrs Stowe loses by it the most terribly tragic element in the relation of the two races – the Nemesis lurking in the vices of the oppressed. She alludes to demoralization among the slaves, but she does not depict it; and yet why should she shrink from this, since she does not shrink from giving us a full-length portrait of a Legree or a Tom Gordon?

It would be idle to tell anything about the story of a work which is, or soon will be, in all our readers' hands; we only render our tribute to it as a great novel, leaving to others the task of weighing it in the political balance.

Close upon *Dred* we have read Mr Charles Reade's novel – *It is Never Too Late to Mend*; also a remarkable fiction, and one that sets vibrating very deep chords in our nature, yet presenting a singular contrast with *Dred*, both in manner and in the essential qualities it indicates in the writer. Mr Reade's novel opens with some of the true pathos to be found in English country life: the honest young farmer, George Fielding, unable to struggle against

'bad times' and an exhausted farm, is driven to Australia
to seek the fortune that will enable him to marry Susan
Merton, the woman he loves. It then carries us, with a
certain Robinson, a clever thief, who has been rusticating
as George Fielding's lodger, to the gaol, and makes us
shudder at the horrors of the separate and silent system,
administered by an ignorant and brutal gaoler, while we
follow with keen interest the struggle of the heroic chap-
lain against this stupid iniquity – thus bringing home the
tragedy of Birmingham gaol to people whose sympathies
are more easily roused by fiction than by bare fact. Then
it takes us to Australia, and traces George Fielding's fortunes and misfortunes – first through the vicissitudes of
the Australian 'sheep-run', and then through the fierce
drama of gold-digging – bringing him home at last with
£4,000 in his pocket, in time to prevent his Susan from
marrying his worst enemy.

In all the three 'acts' of this novel, so to speak, there
are fine situations, fine touches of feeling, and much forcible writing; especially while the scene is in the gaol, the
best companion who drops in you will probably regard as
a bore, and will become earnest in inviting to remain
only when you perceive he is determined to go. Again,
honest George Fielding's struggles, renewed at the antipo-
des, and lightened by the friendship of Carlo the dog – of
the reformed thief, Robinson – and of the delightful
'Jacky', the Australian native – are a thread of interest
which you pursue with eagerness to the *dénouement*.
'Jacky' is a thoroughly fresh character, entirely unlike any
other savage *frotté de civilisation*, and drawn with exquisite yet sober humour. In the English scenes every one

who has seen anything of life amongst our farmers will recognize many truthful, well-observed touches: the little 'tiff' between the brothers George and William Fielding, old Merton's way of thinking, and many traits of manner in the heroine, Susan Merton. In short, *It is Never Too Late to Mend* is one of the exceptional novels to be read not merely by the idle and the half-educated, but by the busy and the thoroughly informed.

Nevertheless, Mr Reade's novel does not rise above the level of cleverness: we feel throughout the presence of remarkable talent, which makes effective use of materials, but nowhere of the genius which absorbs material, and reproduces it as a living whole, in which you do not admire the ingenuity of the workman, but the vital energy of the producer. Doubtless there is a great deal of nonsense talked about genius and inspiration, as if genius did not and must not labour; but, after all, there remains the difference between the writer who thoroughly possesses you by his creation, and the writer who only awakens your curiosity and makes you recognize his ability; and this difference may as well be called 'genius' as anything else. Perhaps a truer statement of the difference is, that the one writer is himself thoroughly possessed by his creation – he lives *in* his characters; while the other remains outside them, and dresses them up. Here lies the fundamental contrast between Mrs Stowe's novel and Mr Reade's. Mrs Stowe seems for the moment to glow with all the passion, to quiver with all the fun, and to be inspired with all the trust that belongs to her different characters; she attains her finest dramatic effects by means of her energetic sympathy, and not by conscious artifice. Mr Reade, on the contrary, seems always self-conscious, always elaborating a character, after a certain type, and carrying his elaboration a little too far – always working up to situations, and over-doing them. The habit of writing for the stage misleads him into seeking after those exaggerated contrasts and effects which are accepted as a sort of rapid symbolism by a theatrical audience, but are utterly out of place in a fiction, where the time and means for attaining a result are less limited, and an impression of character or purpose may be given more nearly as it is in real life – by a sum of less concentrated particulars. In Mr Reade's dialogue we are constantly imagining that we see a theatrical gentleman, well 'made up', delivering a repartee in an emphatic voice, with his eye fixed on the pit. To mention one brief example: – Hawes, the gaoler, tells Fry, the turnkey, after Mr Eden's morning sermon on *theft*, that he approves of preaching *at* people. The same day there is an afternoon sermon on *cruelty*; whereupon Hawes remarks again to Fry, 'I'll teach him to preach at people from the pulpit.' 'Well,' answers Fry, 'that is what I say, Sir: but you said you liked him to preach at folk?' 'So I do,' replied Hawes, angrily, 'but not at me, ye fool!' This would produce a roar on the stage, and would seem a real bit of human nature; but in a novel one has time to be sceptical as to this extreme *naïveté* which allows a man to make palpable epigrams on himself.

In everything, Mr Reade seems to distrust the effect of moderation and simplicity. His picture of gaol life errs by excess, and he wearies our emotion by taxing it too repeatedly; the admirable inspiration which led him to find his hero and heroine among Berkshire homesteads, is counteracted by such puerile and incongruous efforts at the romantic and diabolical, as the introduction of the Jew, Isaac Levi, who is a mosaic character in more senses than one, and the far-seeing Machiavelianism of the top-booted Mr Meadows; and even when he is speaking in his own person, he lashes himself into fury at human wrongs, and calls on God and man to witness his indignation, apparently confounding the importance of the effect with the importance of the cause. But the most amazing foible in a writer of so much power as Mr Reade, is his reliance on the magic of typography. We had imagined that the notion of establishing a relation between magnitude of ideas and magnitude of type was confined to the literature of placards, but we find Mr Reade endeavouring to impress us with the Titanic character of modern events by suddenly bursting into capitals at the mention of 'THIS GIGANTIC AGE!' It seems ungrateful in us to notice these minor blemishes in a work which has given us so much pleasure, and roused in us so much healthy feeling as *It is Never Too Late to Mend*; but it is our very admiration of Mr Reade's talent which makes these blemishes vexatious to us, and which induces us to appeal against their introduction in the many other books we hope to have from his pen.

The appearance of a new novel by Miss Bremer, revives the impressions of ten years ago, when all the novel-reading world was discussing the merits of *The Neighbours, The President's Daughters, The H— Family*, and the rest of the 'Swedish novels', which about that time were creating a strong current in the literary and book-selling world. The discussion soon died out; and perhaps there is hardly another instance of fictions so eagerly read in England which have left so little trace in English literature as Miss Bremer's. No one quotes them, no one alludes to them: and grave people who have entered on their fourth decade, remember their enthusiasm for the Swedish novels among those intellectual 'wild oats' to which their mature wisdom can afford to give a pitying smile. And yet, how is this? For Miss Bremer had not only the advantage of describing manners which were fresh to the English public; she also brought to the description unusual gifts – lively imagination, poetic feeling, wealth of language, a quick eye for details, and considerable humour, of that easy, domestic kind which throws a pleasant light on every-day things. The perusal of *Hertha* has confirmed in our minds the answer we should have previously given to our own question. One reason, we think, why Miss Bremer's novels have not kept a high position among us is, that her luxuriant faculties are all over-run by a rank growth of sentimentality, which, like some faint-smelling creeper on the boughs of an American forest, oppresses us with the sense that the air is unhealthy. Nothing can be more curious than the combination in her novels of the vapourishly affected and unreal with the most solid Dutch sort of realism. In one page we have copious sausage sandwiches and beer posset, and on another rhapsodies or wildly improbable incidents that seem rather to belong to sylphs and salamanders, than to a race of creatures who are nourished by the very excellent provisions just mentioned. Another reason why Miss Bremer's novels are not likely to take rank among the permanent creations of art, is the too confident tone of the religious philosophy which runs through them. When a novelist is quite sure that she has a theory which suffices to illustrate all the difficulties of our earthly existence, her novels are too likely to illustrate little else than her own theory.

These two characteristics of sentimentality and dogmatic confidence are very strongly marked in *Hertha*, while it has less of the attention to detail, less of the humorous realism, which was the ballast of Miss Bremer's earlier novels. It has been written not simply from an artistic impulse, but with the object of advocating the liberation of women from those legal and educational restrictions which limit her opportunities of a position and a sphere of usefulness to the chance of matrimony; and we think there are few well-judging persons who will not admire the generous energy with which Miss Bremer, having long ago won fame and independence for herself, devotes the activity of her latter years to the cause of women who are less capable of mastering circumstance. Many wise and noble things she says in *Hertha*, but we cannot help regretting that she has not presented her views on a difficult and practical question in the 'light of common day', rather than in the pink haze of visions and romance. The story is very briefly this: –

Hertha, who has lost her mother in childhood, is, at the age of seven-and-twenty, becoming more and more embittered by her inactive bondage to a narrow-minded, avaricious father, who demands obedience to the pettiest exactions. Her elder sister, Alma, is slowly dying in consequence of the same tyranny, which has prevented her from marrying the man she loves. We meet our heroine, with her gloomy and bitter expression of face, first of all, at the rehearsal of a fancy ball, which is to take place in a few days in the good town of Kungsköping; and after being introduced to the various *dramatis personæ* – among the rest, to a young man named Yngve Nordin, who interests Hertha by his agreement in her opinions about women, we accompany her to her cheerless home, where she is roughly chid by her father, the rigid old Director, for being later than the regulation-hour of eight; and where, by the bedside of her sister Alma, she pours out all the bitterness of her soul, all her hatred and smothered rebellion towards her father for his injustice towards them. She and Alma have inherited a share in their mother's fortune, but according to the Swedish law they are still minors, and unable to claim their property. This very night, however, a fire breaks out, and lays waste a large district of the town. The Director's house is consumed, and he himself is only saved by the heroic exertions of Hertha, who rushes to his room, and carries his meagre, feeble body through the flames. This act of piety, and the death of Alma, who, in her last moments, extracts from her father a promise to give Hertha independence, win some ungracious concessions from the crabbed Director towards his daughter. He still withholds her property and a declaration of her majority; but she has power in the household, and greater freedom of action out of doors. A Ladies' Society has been organized for relieving the sufferers from the fire, and Hertha is one of those whose department is the care of the sick and wounded. The patient who falls to her share is no other than Yngve Nordin, who has been severely hurt in his benevolent efforts on the fatal night, and is now lodged in the house of the good pastor, who is at the head of the Society. Here is an excellent opportunity for discovering that Yngve is just the friend she needs to soothe and invigorate her mind, by his sympathy and riper experience; and the feeling which is at first called friendship, is at last confessed to be love. After certain jealousies and suspicions, which are satisfactorily cleared up, Yngve asks the Director for Hertha's hand, but is only accepted prospectively, on condition of his attaining an assured position. Yngve goes abroad, and for seven years Hertha submits to the procrastination of her marriage, rather than rebel against her father in his last years. It is only when Yngve is hopelessly ill that she sacrifices her scruples and marries him. In the mean time she has made her seven years of separation rich in active usefulness, by founding and superintending two schools – one in which girls are instructed in the ordinary elements of education, forming a sort of nursery-garden for the other, in which voluntary pupils are to be led to a higher order of thought and purpose by Hertha's readings, conversation, and personal influence. Her schools are successful; but after Yngve's death she begins to sink under her long trial, and follows him rapidly to the grave.

This bare outline of the story can only suggest and not fully explain the grounds of our objection to *Hertha*. Our objection is, that it surrounds questions, which can only be satisfactorily solved by the application of very definite ideas to specific facts, with a cloudy kind of eloquence and flighty romance. Take, for example, the question whether it will not be well for women to study and practise medicine. It can only tend to retard the admission that women may pursue such a career with success, for a distinguished authoress to imply that they may be suitably prepared for effective activity by lectures on such a very nebulous thesis as this – 'The consciousness of thought ought to be a living observation and will', or to associate the attendance of women by the sick-bed, not with the hard drudgery of real practice, but with the vicissitudes of a love-story. Women have not to prove that they can be emotional, and rhapsodic, and spiritualistic; every one believes that already. They have to prove that they are capable of accurate thought, severe study, and continuous self-command. But we say all this with reluctance, and should prefer noticing the many just and pathetic observations that Miss Bremer puts into the mouth of her heroine. We can only mention, and have not space to quote, a passage where Hertha complains of the ignorance in which women are left of Natural Science. 'In my youth,' she concludes, 'I used to look at the rocks, the trees, the grass, and all objects of nature, with unspeakable longing, wishing to know something about their kinds, their life, and their purpose. But the want of knowledge, the want of opportunity to acquire it, has caused nature to be to me a sealed book, and still to this moment it is to me a tantalizing, enticing, and ever-retreating wave, rather than a life-giving fountain which I can enjoy, and enjoying, thank the Creator.'

Translations and Translators

A clergyman (of the Charles Honeyman species) once told us that he never set about preparing his sermons till Saturday evening, for he 'trusted to Providence'. A similar kind of trust, we suppose, must be prevalent among translators, for many of them are evidently relying on some power which

> Can teach all people to translate,
> Though out of languages in which
> They understand no part of speech –

a *Nachklang*, or resonance, perhaps, of the famous legend about those early translators, the Seventy who turned the Old Testament into Greek, which legend tells how Ptolemy shut them up in separate cells to do their work, and how, when they came to compare their renderings, there was perfect agreement! We are convinced, however, that the translators of the Septuagint had some understanding of their business to begin with, or this supernatural aid would not have been given, for in the matter of translation, at least, we have observed, that 'God helps them who help themselves.' A view of the case, which we commend to all young ladies and some middle-aged gentlemen, who consider a very imperfect acquaintance with their own language, and an anticipatory acquaintance with the foreign language, quite a sufficient equipment for the office of translator.

It is perfectly true that, though geniuses have often undertaken translation, translation does not often demand genius. The power required in the translation varies with the power exhibited in the original work: very modest qualifications will suffice to enable a person to translate a book of ordinary travels, or a slight novel, while a work of reasoning or science can be adequately rendered only by means of what is at present exceptional faculty and exceptional knowledge. Among books of this latter kind, Kant's *Critique of Pure Reason* is perhaps the very hardest nut – the peachstone – for a translator to crack so as to lay open the entire uninjured kernel of meaning, and we are glad at last to believe that a translator of adequate power has been employed upon it. For so far as we have examined the version placed at the head of our article, it appears to us very different indeed from the many renderings of German metaphysical works, in which the translator, having ventured into deep waters without learning to swim, clings to the dictionary, and commends himself to Providence. Mr Meiklejohn's translation – so far, we must again observe, as we have examined it – indicates a real mastery of his author, and, for the first time, makes Kant's *Critik der reinen Vernunft* accessible to English readers.

It may seem odd that we should associate with this mighty book – this terrible ninety-gun ship – such a little painted pleasure-boat as Miss (or Mrs) Burt's miscellaneous collection of translations from German lyric poets. But we are concerning ourselves here simply with translation –

not at all with Kant's philosophy or with German lyrics considered in themselves, and these two volumes happen to be the specimens of translation most recently presented to our notice. With regard to prose, we may very generally use Goldsmith's critical recipe, and say that the translation would have been better if the translator had taken more pains; but of poetical attempts we are often sure that no amount of pains would produce a satisfactory result. And so it is with Miss Burt's *Specimens of the German Poets*. She appears to have the knowledge and the industry which many translators want, but she has not the poetic power which makes poetical translations endurable to those acquainted with the originals. Amongst others, however, who have no such acquaintance, Miss Burt's translations seem to have been in some demand, since they have reached a second edition. She has been bold enough to attempt a version of Goethe's exquisite *Zueignung* (*Dedication*), and here is a specimen of her rendering. Goethe sings with divine feeling and music –

> Für andre wächst in mir das edle Gut,
> Ich kann und will das Pfund nicht mehr vergraben,
> Warum sucht' ich den Weg so sehnsuchtsvoll,
> Wenn ich ihn nicht den Brüdern zeigen soll?

Miss Burt follows him much as a Jew's harp would follow a piano –

> Entombed no longer shall my *talent* be,
> That treasure I amass, shall others share?

> To find the road – oh, why such zeal display,
> If I guide not my brethren on their way?

A version like this bears about the same relation to the original as the portraits in an illustrated newspaper bear to the living face of the distinguished gentlemen they misrepresent; and considering how often we hear opinions delivered on foreign poets by people who only know those poets at second hand, it becomes the reviewer's duty to insist again and again on the inadequacy of poetic translations.

The Germans render our poetry better than we render theirs, for their language, as slow and unwieldy as their own post-horses in prose, becomes in poetry graceful and strong and flexible as an Arabian war-horse. Besides, translation among them is more often undertaken by men of genius. We remember, for example, some translations of Burns, by Freiligrath, which would have arrested us by their beauty if we had seen the poems for the first time, in this language. It is true the Germans think a little too highly of their translations, and especially are under the illusion, encouraged by some silly English people, that Shakspeare according to Schlegel is better than Shakspeare himself – not simply better to a German as being easier for him to understand, but absolutely better as poetry. A very close and admirable rendering Schlegel's assuredly is, and it is a high pleasure to track it in its faithful adherence to the original, just as it is to examine a fine engraving of a favourite picture. Sometimes the German is as good as the English – the same music played on another but as good an instrument. But more frequently the German is a feeble echo, and here and there it breaks down in a supremely fine passage. An instance of this kind occurs in the famous speech of Lorenzo to Jessica. Shakspeare says –

> Soft stillness and the night
> Become the touches of sweet harmony.

This Schlegel renders –

> Sanfte Still und Nacht
> Sie werden *Tasten* süsser Harmonie.

That is to say, 'Soft stillness and the night *are* the *finger-board* of sweet harmony.' A still worse blunder is made by Tieck (whose translation is the rival of Schlegel's) in the monologue of Macbeth. In the lines –

> That but this blow
> Might be the be-all and the end-all here –
> But here upon this bank and shoal of time,
> I'd jump the life to come –

Tieck renders, 'Upon this bank and shoal of time', 'Auf dieser *Schülerbank* der Gegenwart', that is, 'On this *school-bench* of the present!' These are cases of gross inaccuracy arising from an imperfect understanding of the original. Here is an instance of feebleness. Coriolanus says –

> And like an eagle in the dovecote, I
> Flutter'd the Volscians in Corioli.

For the admirably descriptive word 'fluttered', Schlegel gives *schlug*, which simply means 'slew'. Weak renderings of this kind are abundant.

Such examples of translators' fallibility in men like Schlegel and Tieck might well make less accomplished persons more backward in undertaking the translation of great poems, and by showing the difficulty of the translator's task, might make it an object of ambition to real ability. Though a good translator is infinitely below the man who produces *good* original works, he is infinitely above the man who produces *feeble* original works. We had meant to say something of the moral qualities especially demanded in the translator – the patience, the rigid fidelity, and the sense of responsibility in interpreting another man's mind. But we have gossiped on this subject long enough.

THE STORY OF PENGUIN CLASSICS

Before 1946 ... 'Classics' are mainly the domain of academics and students; readable editions for everyone else are almost unheard of. This all changes when a little-known classicist, E. V. Rieu, presents Penguin founder Allen Lane with the translation of Homer's *Odyssey* that he has been working on in his spare time.

1946 Penguin Classics debuts with *The Odyssey*, which promptly sells three million copies. Suddenly, classics are no longer for the privileged few.

1950s Rieu, now series editor, turns to professional writers for the best modern, readable translations, including Dorothy L. Sayers's *Inferno* and Robert Graves's unexpurgated *Twelve Caesars*.

1960s The Classics are given the distinctive black covers that have remained a constant throughout the life of the series. Rieu retires in 1964, hailing the Penguin Classics list as 'the greatest educative force of the twentieth century.'

1970s A new generation of translators swells the Penguin Classics ranks, introducing readers of English to classics of world literature from more than twenty languages. The list grows to encompass more history, philosophy, science, religion and politics.

1980s The Penguin American Library launches with titles such as *Uncle Tom's Cabin*, and joins forces with Penguin Classics to provide the most comprehensive library of world literature available from any paperback publisher.

1990s The launch of Penguin Audiobooks brings the classics to a listening audience for the first time, and in 1999 the worldwide launch of the Penguin Classics website extends their reach to the global online community.

The 21st Century Penguin Classics are completely redesigned for the first time in nearly twenty years. This world-famous series now consists of more than 1300 titles, making the widest range of the best books ever written available to millions – and constantly redefining what makes a 'classic'.

The Odyssey continues ...

The best books ever written

PENGUIN CLASSICS

SINCE 1946

Find out more at www.penguinclassics.com